CATEGORY: TEAM WORK

Your people - an employer's guide to effective people management

By John McManus

Edited by Andrew Steeds

```
DRS BRAY, SMITH, PATEL
TANNA & WHITER
St. Andrews Medical Practice
50 Oakleigh Road North
Whetstone London N20 9EX
Tel: 020 8445 0475
```

INVESTORS IN
PEOPLE UK

Published by Investors in People UK
7–10 Chandos Street
London W1M 9DE
Tel +44 (0)171 467 1900
Fax +44(0)171 636 2386
E-mail: information@iipuk.co.uk
Website: www.iipuk.co.uk

© John McManus 1994, 1999

First published as *Keeping The Team In Shape* by the Institute of Personnel and Development in 1994

This edition first published 1999
Editor Andrew Steeds

Typesetting Creation Communication Design Limited

Cover design The Workroom

Printed and bound by Jarrold Book Printing

British Library Cataloguing in Publication Data

A catalogue record for this book is available from the British Library

ISBN 1-900567-06-7

Building a better business and the associated circular logo device are the intellectual property of Investors in People UK and Scottish Enterprise and may only be reproduced with the express permission of these parties. Breach of copyright will result in legal action being taken.

The Building a better business mark and logo are protected by trademark law and may not be used save for prior written permission from Investors in People UK and Scottish Enterprise.

contents

About this book	1

1 The bare minimum

Doing without employees	2
Part-time workers	3
Recruitment	5
Formality and forms	8

2 ill-health and injury

Introduction	17
Absence records	18
Sick pay	19
Repeated absence and long-term sickness	23

3 Pregnancy and maternity benefits

Antenatal care	27
Maternity leave	30
Statutory Maternity Pay	32
Maternity Allowance	34

4 Holidays and time off

Holidays	36
Other absences	39

5 Discipline, the groundwork

Keeping it formal	43
Local rules	44
Management's role in discipline	46
Disciplinary remedies	48

6 Incompetence and misconduct

Sub-standard work	55
Health and hygiene problems	57
Office affairs	59
Misconduct and remedies	61

7 Fair and unfair dismissals

Introduction	67
Constructive dismissal	69
Negotiated departures	70
Disputed exits and the industrial tribunal	72

8 Redundancy

The cost of redundancy	76
Minimum notice periods	79
Selection for redundancy	80
Underlying reasons for redundancy	82
Employer's duty to minimise effects	84

9 Useful addresses

	86

about this book

The owners of most small organisations are likely to have worked for other people at some time, generally in much larger organisations. In the process, they will have met personnel managers and maybe training managers, industrial relations managers and the rest of the experts that a large business can afford to carry.

The key phrase there, of course, is 'can afford to carry'. If any business is to survive and thrive, it must keep its overheads to an absolute minimum. And even if you have decided, for that reason (or maybe because your business is smaller), to do without such people, you are nevertheless likely to find yourself having to *perform their functions*.

In other words, if you have decided not to employ specific people for these roles, you will probably have to be your own personnel manager, your own industrial relations manager. Even if you hire someone else to cover the basic aspects of these functions, you will still need to understand fully what is involved: you will, after all, be the first point of contact and the main point of referral.

This activity need only take up a small amount of your time – provided that you do a small number of things reasonably well and at the right time. You don't need any great technical skill for any of these functions (you don't need much more than common sense for most of them) – but, if you ignore the need altogether, you will be storing up a source of potential trouble.

This book sets out to examine what these essential functions are. In the process it aims to do four things:

- to identify the routines you need to get right;
- to tell you how to install them, easily, quickly and cheaply;
- to explain what may happen if you don't bother to do so;
- to outline what can and cannot be done, should something go wrong.

A number of organisations are listed in the Useful Addresses section at the end of this book. This list is not intended to be exhaustive, and there will inevitably be other organisations that individual businesses need to contact. Addresses and telephone numbers of organisations listed are correct at the time of publication.

Your People – an employer's guide to effective people management is part of the *Building a Better Business* range of materials, produced to meet the needs of smaller, developing organisations. Core to this range is a practical business development tool kit, which pulls together all the disciplines of good business management.

The books in the range have been produced as practical, self contained resources, which can be taken on their own or, used to supplement the individual sections from the tool kit.

All materials in the range are published by Investors in People UK.

1 the bare minimum

DOING WITHOUT EMPLOYEES

The only certain way to avoid all liability for employees is not to have any, or, at least, not to have anybody who qualifies as an employee. For example, if your business needs sales representatives, why not ask them to be self-employed? They can supply their own transport, look after their own National Insurance (NI) affairs, and you can pay them on commission only. It's an arrangement that sounds neat and tidy and prevents you having to pay the employer's NI contributions.

If you run your business in this way, both the Inland Revenue and the Department of Social Security may take exception to the arrangement. They may argue, through the courts if necessary, that the arrangement is contrived and that the people involved are in fact employees, whatever you or your employees may say to the contrary.

Establishing self-employed status

There is no unequivocal, legal definition of employment. However, there is a test the courts use to establish whether someone is in fact self-employed, and it involves asking the following kind of questions:

- Who controls the manner, time and place of work?
- Who provides the premises, tools and equipment?
- Who takes the financial risk?
- Who takes the chance of profit?
- Is the person involved working on their own account?
- Are they integrated in the business, e.g. does the employer grant sickness and/or holiday entitlement?
- Who pays the NI contributions and income tax?

- Is there any form of contract which describes the people involved as employee and employer?
- Is there just the one contract, or is the person contracted with various other businesses?

If the sales representatives used in the example above are, in reality, working full time for your company, it is very likely that it will emerge from their answers to these questions. On the other hand, if they are representing several different and unconnected companies at the same time and collecting commission from all of them, they can qualify as self-employed. In effect, they will have their own businesses.

The penalties of getting it wrong

Unless you are confident you can prove the self-employed status of the people who work for you, it's a dangerous game to play, and the penalties for getting it wrong may be harsh. Employers have a duty to deduct income tax at source: if they fail to do so, the liability for outstanding tax can become the employers' rather than the employees'. The same is true of National Insurance, where employers have the additional burden of the employer's NI contribution. There may also be penalties imposed for the incorrect collection of State taxes.

PART-TIME WORKERS

Many businesses depend on part-time workers. It's a convenient, flexible way to operate for both parties. Depending on the hours worked and the rates of pay, the employer can legally avoid paying an employer's NI contribution and, of course, the administrative bother of NI deductions from the employee's wages. This is only possible below the lower earnings limit for NI purposes. A telephone call to your local DSS office will confirm the current level if you are uncertain.

the bare minimum

As far as income tax is concerned, there is a threshold below which there is no liability (information about the current level is available from your tax office). What you need to do is:

- ask the part-timer to complete an Inland Revenue form P46 when they join, confirming that this is their main job;
- add a few bits of information identifying the employing company;
- either send it to the tax office or, where payment is very low, retain it for future proof.

It's a simple enough form. The few minutes it takes you to fill it in will set the seal on your non-liability to deduct tax below the earnings limit. However, where the job is *not* the employee's main job, you *must* deduct tax at the basic rate from the outset.

In general, part-time employees have the same rights as full-time employees if:

- they work more than sixteen hours per week, or
- they have worked between eight and sixteen hours per week and have been with you for at least five years.

But even those working fewer than sixteen hours have the same unfair-dismissal and redundancy rights as full-time employees. This is highly significant. For the purposes of redundancy, for example, part-timers' service will be considered to be continuous. And, unless you specified holiday pay or sickness benefits when the part-timer joined, they would have the same entitlement as any full-timer.

Remember, also, that employers' liability insurance is needed the moment you employ your first person – whether they are part time or full time.

RECRUITMENT

Recruitment is outside the scope of this book (it is discussed in detail in *Your People – an employer's guide to recruitment and selection,* also published by Investors in People UK), but it needs to be mentioned here because insufficient care taken at the time of recruitment is the cause of a high proportion of the problems that arise with staff management. This is true regardless of the level at which people are being recruited. Indeed, it's probably easier to recruit a Chartered Accountant than a part-time shop assistant: the former's history will be well documented; there will be half a dozen or so sources for you to go to for confirmation that the applicant is what they claim to be. Contrast this with someone who has not worked for anyone in the last fifteen years and is responding to an advertisement in a shop window.

The best way to prevent problems is to anticipate and pre-empt them, and the first stage in this process should be a short, simple application form: an example is given opposite. There are three advantages in this kind of formality:

- It's a rough and ready proof that the person concerned can read and write
- It will tell you where else they have worked, in what capacity and for how long – a telephone call will confirm or deny this information
- The applicant will have signed it.

This last point may be the most important. If you find out, later on, that your employee has deliberately misled you, you will have absolute proof in your possession – and you can then decide what to do about it. That's a lot better than trying to remember and, worse, *prove* what was said at the interview.

the bare minimum

APPLICATION FOR EMPLOYMENT
Concise Form

Please return completed form to:

APPLICANT — Please complete in INK using BLOCK CAPITALS PRIVATE & CONFIDENTIAL

- Forename(s)
- Surname
- Previous Surname(s)
- Home Address
- Postcode

Position applied for

Enclosed with this Application form (tick as applicable)
- [ ] Job Description
- [ ] Occupational Health Assessment / Screening Questionnaire (Pre-employment)

Employment: Place(s) of work: [ ] At address given above
- Full-time / Part-time &/or [ ]
- Permanent / Temporary
Delete N/A Applicable

- Tel. No. (home)
- E-mail address (home)
- Tel. No. (work)
- Date of Birth / /
- If you are shortlisted, you will be asked to produce a 'specified document' (e.g. a P60, NINO card, UK or Eire birth certificate, passport) confirming your eligibility to live and work in the UK in accordance with the Asylum and Immigration Act 1996 - Section 8.
- Would you be able to produce such a document? YES / NO
- Would you have to move home if offered this job? YES / NO
- Do you have a current clean driving licence? YES / NO
- For what classes of vehicle?

OPTIONAL QUESTIONS in this shaded area. *Please see declaration on reverse.*

Ethnic Origin
For the purpose of monitoring census data, please indicate the ethnic group to which you belong. Ethnic origin is not about nationality, place of birth or citizenship; it concerns colour and broad ethnic group.
(tick box)
- [ ] White
- [ ] Bangladeshi
- [ ] Indian
- [ ] Pakistani
- [ ] Black African
- [ ] Black Caribbean
- [ ] Black Other (specify)
- [ ] Chinese
- [ ] Other Asian (state)
- [ ] Other (state)

- No. of penalty points (if any) endorsed on current driving licence
- Have you ever had your driving licence revoked? YES / NO
- Your living accommodation, e.g. owner occupied house, rented flat, living with parents

GENERAL EDUCATION

Secondary Education			Further Education		
From	To	Name of school	From	To	Name of college, university etc.
/	/		/	/	
/	/		/	/	

Examination results/qualifications obtained

EMPLOYMENT

Name and address of current employer (or last employer if not currently employed)	Job title and main duties	Employment Dates	
		From	To
		/	/

Average gross pay £ _____ per week / month / annum   Reason for leaving

Previous employment (employer name and your job title)
1. _____ / / — / /
2. _____ / / — / /
3. _____ / / — / /

HEALTH

| Height | | Weight | | Would you be willing to have a medical examination if required? YES / NO |

OPTIONAL QUESTIONS in this shaded area. *Please see declaration on reverse.*

Do you smoke? YES / NO If YES, give details _____
of past and present tobacco usage

Are you currently receiving any medical treatment? YES / NO
If YES, give details

Note: If we have sent you a separate Occupational Health form, please complete and post it to the Medical Advisor in an envelope marked 'Strictly Private & Confidential'. (Note to Employer - see Chancellor Formecon form ref. FS.35)

This form is reproduced with the permission of the copyright holder and publisher, Formecon Services Ltd, Crewe.

6

Taking up references

It is always worth taking up references, and probably best to do so over the phone: employers tend to be much more guarded in writing. Here are some suggestions about the form this sort of call should take:

- Try to ensure that the referee was the candidate's immediate boss. The higher up the tree you go, the less that person will really know about the ex-employee.
- Lead the conversation yourself. Quote what you've been told about dates, job titles, etc. and ask for confirmation.
- Don't expect a statement encapsulating all you need to know in a few carefully constructed sentences.
- Encourage the person you are speaking to: give them leads such as 'Sarah and I had quite a long chat. She struck me as being rather shy: a nervous sort of girl. Do you think that's right?'
- Put your enquiry into context. For example: 'It's a trade counter, in effect. She'll have to put up with a parts system on a PC and drivers turning up with scruffy, almost indecipherable pieces of paper and a strong line in chat-up phrases. How do you think she'll cope? Is this the sort of system you use?'

This technique is helpful to referees because they will not feel that they are doing all the work. As a result, they are more likely to relax, and you will get more help from them. In general, the more information you seem to be giving, the more you'll get in return.

Before moving on, one further recruitment suggestion is worth mentioning. Many companies, sometimes very large ones, go out of their way to encourage their staff to recruit for them, even to the extent of offering small bonuses for successful introductions. There are a number of good reasons for this practice:

the bare minimum

- It reduces or cuts out altogether the need for, and the cost of, recruitment advertising
- Candidates will be known quantities to staff members, who can be quizzed about them
- The introducing employee will feel responsible for the candidate and tend to believe that any failure or incompetence will reflect on them too.

There's a lot to be said for this technique, but there are also potential problems (for example, your employee may have been bullied into recommending a useless relative) – these are discussed in greater detail in *Your People – an employer's guide to recruitment and selection*.

FORMALITY AND FORMS

This section proposes a pragmatic, legal way in which to deal with personnel paperwork with minimal effort on your part. Ideally, you would do more, but this approach assumes you have limited time at your disposal.

The system depends on the use of just three forms. You don't need to design any of them – you can buy them from Chancellor Formecon, cheaply, in small quantities, ready-printed on NCR (no carbon required) paper so that you get an immediate copy of the original (see Useful Addresses, p. 86). Each form is a checklist in itself. The headings are generally supported by clear notes, on the reverse, which explain what they are all about for the benefit of employer and employee.

The three forms are as follows:

- Application for Employment
- Statement of Employment Particulars
- Employer's Rules and Procedures.

The application form and the reasons for its use have been dealt with already. It is very important that you understand the need for the remaining two forms. Each of these will now be dealt with in turn.

Statement of employment particulars

All employees who work more than eight hours per week are entitled to receive what is popularly called a contract of employment within two months of the date on which employment commenced. In fact, what they are due is a *Statement of Employment Particulars*.

Employers in small or medium-sized businesses often do not bother to issue this document, yet nothing seems to happen as a result. So, why not simply ignore the thing altogether?

The short answer is that you should look on it as a kind of insurance. You'll only ever need it when something has gone wrong, and by that time it will be too late to produce it. That's when you'll wish you had spent a few minutes on it, all that time ago. On the surface it looks as though it is for the employee's benefit, but it provides a great deal of protection for the employer too, especially when they are drawn into a dispute and asked to attend an industrial tribunal.

An example of the pre-printed form mentioned earlier is shown on page 10. Some of the headings used on the form are given on page 11. Read the comments beside them: you'll see that the form provides certainty, for you and your employee. That certainty will be your protection, whereas deliberate vagueness or silence will often militate against you. The bulk of employment law has been constructed for the benefit of employees, not for you. They are always presumed to be at a disadvantage. You, the employer, are supposed to have the greater bargaining power. The employee needs to be protected from you.

the bare minimum

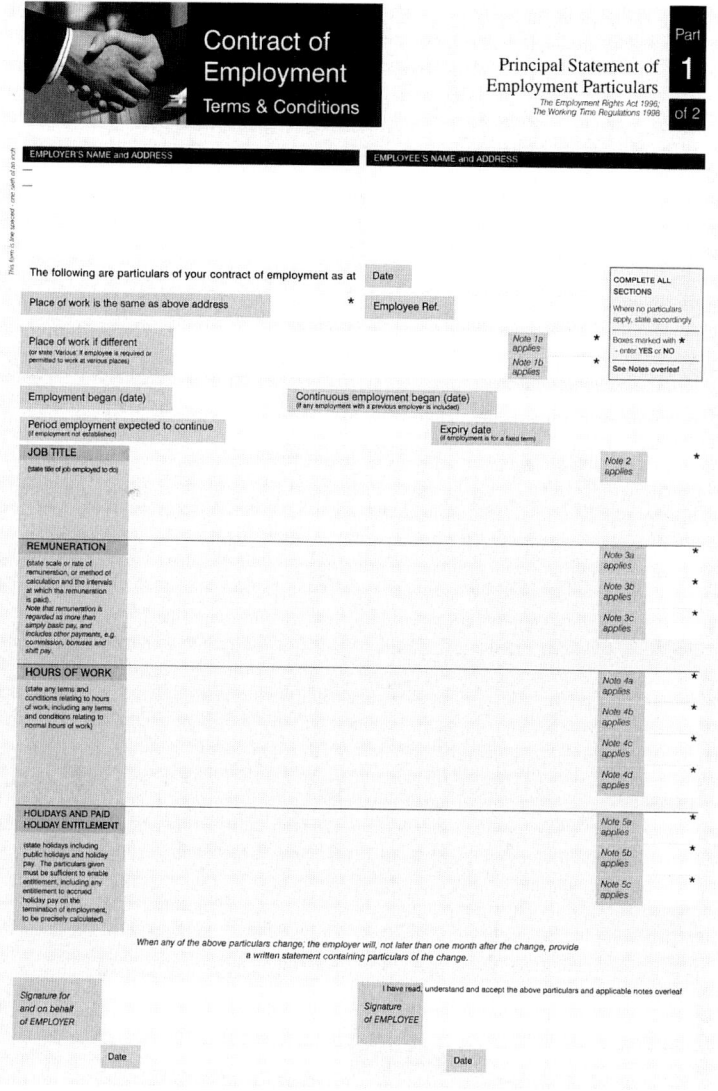

the bare minimum

Job title
If the title does not give a clear indication of the tasks and duties involved, list the main ones. The note on the reverse side of the printed form says 'You will be expected to carry out such other duties as may reasonably be required'. (Think about the muddle you might get into with an employee who refused to do anything other than their listed activities.)

Remuneration
It is very important to state the basic pay, the payment period (weekly, monthly, quarterly, etc.) and, if there is any commission or bonus, how these elements are calculated. In the event of dismissal, including redundancy, the final pay packet will come under intense scrutiny.

No *new* employee has a right to be paid in cash. You can move existing employees to payment by cheque or to their banks but only with their consent. If you do it without their blessing, you'll be in breach of contract.

Hours of work
If you don't specify what hours the employee is expected to work, it will be difficult to prove lateness! If overtime is a fixed requirement, you need to say so. If you expect extra, unpaid hours from time to time, you can rely on the notes on the reverse of the printed form. If you engage a night-shift worker, do not assume you'll always have a night shift. Allow yourself maximum flexibility (otherwise, for example, you might end up paying a night-shift premium for day work).

Holidays and holiday pay
There is no legal entitlement to paid holidays for anyone. Contrary to common belief, even bank holidays aren't automatic. State how many days, including bank holidays, you are allowing and whether you intend to pay all or any of the holiday days. Specify the way in which pay will be calculated, eg at the basic hourly rate for a theoretical eight-hour day.

the bare minimum

Sickness

The forms referred to earlier carry notes concerning Statutory Sick Pay (SSP) and certificates. You need to state whether or not there is an entitlement to any topping up of wages above SSP. If there is, set out the rules: e.g. no entitlement in the first six months of service and thereafter at the management's discretion – or whatever formula you settle on. Be clear as to how you intend to calculate sick pay, too. Don't forget that, if you say nothing, your custom and practice elsewhere may be taken to apply.

Discipline

The disciplinary code is dealt with in more detail later in this book (page 43). It is the third of the forms you'll need.

Notice

If you dismiss an employee or make their job redundant (which amounts to the same thing), you must remember to give the statutory periods of notice that are listed in the chapter on redundancy (see p. 76). If you provide longer periods within your job offer and the Statement of Employment Particulars, these will take precedence.

Grievances

Your procedure for allowing any employee to settle their grievances doesn't have to be elaborate. In a small organisation it might amount to nothing more than 'Speak to the manager about it. If this doesn't resolve the problem, talk to me.' What's important is that you provide this mechanism and that you use it responsibly. If you do so, you will be seen as a thoughtful, reasonable employer.

Pension

Most small companies, if they provide pensions at all, will tend to have a series of individual policies for selected members of staff. For most readers 'not applicable' will suffice. If, however, you have a small, general scheme under which employees join after, say, one year's service, remember to place the onus on them to apply for membership. If you don't – and you've forgotten to invite them to join on time – it may prove very expensive when, after several years, they demand that their membership be backdated.

Contract of Employment

Strictly speaking, a contract of employment is not a document. It is a convenient, legalistic phrase that includes:

- conversations you had with the person concerned, including any inducements offered, before they joined;
- your letter of offer;
- the employee's response, if it included any qualification of your offer;
- subsequent changes accepted by both parties;
- the Statement of Employment Particulars.

For the purpose of this chapter, the important thing to remember is that a contract of employment is more than just the last of these elements.

Employer's rules and procedures

The forms for employer's rules and procedures (shown on pages 14–15) contain what is commonly described as the 'Disciplinary Code'. However, the much less threatening title 'Rules and Procedures' is now the official title.

An employer's reaction to their first encounter with this document is often something like this: 'We don't need to go to these lengths to deal with discipline. We don't have these problems. Ours is a nice, quiet business, employing civilised, reasonable people. Any problems we have are minor, and I can easily sort them out myself.'

That may be so. We all, of course, assume and hope that nothing will go wrong. But none of us can guarantee that nothing will ever go wrong – and if something does, and you have no contract, where is your defence? One very expensive solicitor said to his client, who had just signed a 150-page contract, 'You can put your copy into a drawer somewhere and forget all about it… Until something goes wrong, that is. Then you'll rush to it, read it and suddenly realise that the thousands of pounds it cost you was money very well spent indeed.'

the bare minimum

PERSONNEL MANAGEMENT

EMPLOYER'S
Disciplinary Procedure

Employer Name and Address

This Disciplinary Procedure and your Employers Rules (a copy of which is readily accessible, if not already displayed) are designed to help and encourage all employees to achieve and maintain acceptable levels of conduct, attendance and performance. This Disciplinary Procedure is not contractual, it has been issued in accordance with statutory obligations and should be retained for information and guidance.

When considering disciplinary procedures, the employer will –
1. Take action in a uniform and consistent manner
2. Investigate carefully and hear the employee
3. Wherever reasonably practicable, seek to correct rather than punish
4. Implement procedures on fair grounds
5. Take into account all facts, circumstances and rights before reaching a decision
6. Consider all suitable alternatives
7. Provide employees with the right of appeal at every stage of the procedure.

General Principles

General Principles of the Disciplinary Procedure.

- At each stage of the disciplinary procedure a thorough investigation to establish the facts will be carried out and the employee concerned given an opportunity to state his or her case
- An employee has the right to be accompanied by a work colleague at the disciplinary hearing
- An employee has a right to appeal against any disciplinary penalty imposed
- At every stage of the disciplinary procedure the employee will be advised of the nature of the complaint against him or her
- An employee will not be dismissed for a first breach of discipline except in the case of gross misconduct
- In the event of a disciplinary hearing being held, the management representative will provide the employee concerned with a written record of the hearing
- An employee may be temporarily removed from his/her duties or suspended on full pay whilst investigations are carried out
- The disciplinary procedure may be implemented at any stage if the employee's conduct or performance warrants such action
- Disciplinary action taken will be subject to the following time limits:
  - an oral warning will be disregarded after 6 months
  - a written warning will be disregarded after 12 months.

If, in exceptional circumstances, there is no time limit, or if the time limit is varied, this will be communicated to the employee at the time of the disciplinary action being taken.

Conduct

Misconduct

The following offences are examples of misconduct (this list is not exhaustive)
- unsatisfactory attendance record
- bad time-keeping
- unauthorised absence
- unsatisfactory performance
- output falling below minimum required level
- minor breach of Employer's rules
- failure to comply with the Employer's self-certification scheme
- minor damage to the property occupied by the Employer
- abusive behaviour.

Gross misconduct

The following offences are examples of gross misconduct (this list is not exhaustive)
- fighting, violent, dangerous or intimidating conduct
- theft or unauthorised possession of the Employer's property or another employee's property
- falsification of Employer's forms or medical records
- discrimination on racial grounds, or on grounds of sex, marital status or disability, including harassment
- acceptance of work-related bribes
- serious refusal to carry out a reasonable instruction
- intoxication by reason of drink, drugs or solvents
- serious breach of the Employer's rules or procedures
- gross negligence
- bringing the Employer/Employer's organisation into disrepute
- wilful or serious damage to the Employer's property
- any fraudulent or dishonest act or omission
- any wilful or reckless act constituting a serious danger to the health and safety of any person
- unauthorised disclosure of sensitive or confidential information.

continue overleaf

the bare minimum

The Procedure for Misconduct

Very minor issues may be dealt with informally. Where the matter is more serious the following procedure applies:

Stage 1 - Oral Warning

In the first instance of alleged failure to meet the Employer's standards of conduct or performance a disciplinary hearing will take place with the employee. If, as a result of the hearing, disciplinary action is deemed necessary, then an **oral warning** (see Chancellor® Formecon form ref. FS.708- 'Disciplinary Warning') will be issued in writing to the employee. This will include:-
- A description of the conduct/performance complained of. In a case where improvement is required, the nature of that improvement must be specified and how the employee is expected to achieve this
- The period during which this improvement is expected to take place and the need to sustain the required standard thereafter
- The consequences of failing to improve as required, or of further misconduct
- The employee's right to appeal.

Stage 2 - Written Warning

If the Employer is satisfied after investigation that the standards of performance are not being met in the time period specified in Stage 1, or if there is an alleged recurrence of the misconduct, or if there is a serious alleged failure to meet the Employer's standards of conduct or performance, a disciplinary hearing will take place with the employee. If, as a result of this hearing, disciplinary action is deemed necessary, then a **written warning** will be issued in the format described in Stage 1.

Stage 3 - Final Written Warning

If the Employer is satisfied after investigation that the standards of performance are not being met within the time period specified in Stage 2, or if there is an alleged recurrence of misconduct, or if there is a very serious alleged failure to meet the Employer's standards of conduct or performance, a disciplinary hearing will take place with the employee. If appropriate the final written warning will be issued in the format described in Stage 1. This will confirm that it is a **final written warning** and that further misconduct or insufficient improvement will normally result in dismissal.

Stage 4 - Dismissal

If the Employer is satisfied after investigation that the standards of conduct or performance are not being met within the time period specified in Stage 3, or there is a further alleged recurrence of misconduct, a disciplinary hearing will be called with the employee. If, as a result of this hearing, disciplinary action is deemed necessary the Employer may decide to either dismiss the employee with notice or issue a further final warning if there are special mitigating circumstances with other disciplinary measures to be taken as appropriate. Either outcome should be recorded in writing and issued to the employee.

The Procedure for Gross Misconduct

In all cases of alleged gross misconduct the Employer may temporarily suspend an employee on full pay while investigations are carried out. If, on completion of the investigation and the full disciplinary procedure, the Employer is satisfied that gross misconduct has occurred, the result will normally be summary dismissal without notice or payment in lieu of notice.

Amendments or additions by employer

Appeals Procedure

An employee may appeal against a decision at any stage of the disciplinary procedure. The appeal should be made in writing, setting out the grounds of appeal, to the Employer or a senior member of staff, within five working days of notification of the decision.

FS.703

This form is reproduced with the permission of the copyright holder and publisher, Formecon Services Ltd, Crewe.

15

the bare minimum

These rules and procedures are your first line of defence when something goes wrong. The form itself is pretty self-explanatory: it tells the employee very clearly what you expect of them and is based on the Advisory Conciliation and Arbitration Service (ACAS) Code of Practice, which provides a solid underpinning in terms of its authority and reasonableness.

Placing the responsibility on the employee too

It also places the responsibility on employees to find out for themselves what is or is not acceptable in certain areas. For example, it requires the employee to find out whether private telephone calls, or use of the photocopier, are permissible, and to what extent. If an employee did not bother to find out about matters like this, it will count against them. The same form tells employees that, to take other examples, wilful neglect of health and safety precautions will be regarded as a serious offence or misconduct, and that falsifying time sheets could result in dismissal. Having the form provides certainty and leaves the employee in no doubt as to what you expect of them.

How you apply these rules and procedures when it comes to dismissals will be dealt with in more detail in a later chapter. However, it is worth noting in this context that your role as an employer carries with it one paramount responsibility: once you have issued these rules and procedures, you must use them, too. Read the list of employer's responsibilities at the head of the form. If you ever end up in the arms of an industrial tribunal, the fact that you have carried out your part of the bargain, carefully and reasonably, will stand you in good stead. You'll be like the solicitor's client mentioned earlier: quietly pleased with your foresight.

Any reader requiring more detailed discussion of the process of recruitment from the point of view of interview onwards should consult Chapters 5 and 6 in *Your People – an employer's guide to recruitment and selection*, also published by Investors in People UK.

ill health and injury 2

INTRODUCTION

Contrary to the romantic saying, employee absence does not generally make the employer's heart grow fonder. The smaller the business, the more difficult it is to cope with unforeseen absences.

However inconvenient such absences may be, your reaction should not be to try to work out whether an employee is really sick when they say they are, still less to decide that it's all in their mind. You are bound to accept plausible reasons for absence at face value, unless you have proof to the contrary.

There may come a point, however, when prolonged absence (whatever the reason) causes you to question the viability of keeping on an employee. If you are starting to think in terms of dismissal, the amount of time an employee has worked in your company becomes important. You can dismiss almost any employee during the first two years of service with due notice but without necessarily having to give a reason for dismissal. (There are a few exceptions to this rule – for example dismissing a woman because she is pregnant , which counts as unfair dismissal, or dismissing an employee for activities concerning union membership – and these will be dealt with in later chapters.) If an employee has been with you more than two years, however, you will have to provide reasonable grounds if you are to avoid a charge of unfair dismissal.

As with other issues covered already, the best way of preventing most problems is to ensure that you and your employees are aware of the procedures covering absence and sickness from the outset.

ill health and injury

ABSENCE RECORDS

In any dispute the most important thing is to have the facts to hand. If, for instance, an employee has had what you recall as a considerable number of odd days off in the last twelve months, but you have no absolute record of them, you have a problem. What starts as a reasonable discussion may turn into an argument, with each party relying on their own, sometimes unreliable, memory.

The way to avoid this is to keep records. For the small business, this can be as simple as getting a desk-top diary. Drill a hole through it and suspend it, on a piece of string or whatever, in some obvious place. Ask your staff to sign it each day when they arrive. Once a week, look at it yourself and quickly initial each page. If names are missing, check that the person concerned was out that day. They may, of course, have merely forgotten to sign, in which case make them do so – and nag them, half seriously, so they don't forget next time.

Writing one's name in a diary once a day will not spoil the informal atmosphere that most small businesses pride themselves on. But this system will only work if you make it work. You must spare the time, a few minutes once a week, to check and initial it. If you don't, it will fall into disuse quite quickly. How far you want to carry the routine is up to you. You may choose, for example, to note that last Tuesday Jim was out but called in sick, or that Sarah took Wednesday off as a leave day. The diary will do as much or as little for you as you decide.

If you use this system, you should include everyone in it. Don't make exceptions and don't insist that particular members of staff sign the book. There's no reason why managers and supervisors should not sign. In any area where there are problems associated with people, you will want to be seen as a fair and even-handed employer. So, if you note lateness, note everyone's lateness, not just one individual's. In the process you'll avoid any suggestion that you are picking on one person – something that never goes down well with third parties, especially when the third party is an industrial tribunal.

The desk diary routine is simple and effective, but there are also many, more elaborate, systems available. These range from pre-printed forms (available from Chancellor Formecon, for example – see Useful Addresses, p. 86) to fairly sophisticated software for use on a PC. The average proprietor of the smaller business may not need the level of refinement offered by the latter, but you will need something.

SICK PAY

There is no automatic entitlement for employees to receive any form of sick pay other than that provided under the heading of Statutory Sick Pay (SSP). (Since pregnancy is not an illness, maternity benefits can be disregarded here: they are dealt with separately in the next chapter.) But it is wise not to be complacent about this. In the general area of employment law, silence is not necessarily golden. If you have decided that a more recently recruited person should not enjoy the sick pay that a number of your current employees enjoy, you must say so, preferably in writing. If you say nothing, or affect a deliberate vagueness, and are then hauled off to an industrial tribunal, your custom and practice will be taken into account and you may find yourself having to pay up. Don't be an ostrich, sticking your head in the sand and hoping that the employee will never raise the matter. Assume that it will be raised and deal with it at the outset.

Whether or not you should provide company sick pay is for you to decide. Can you afford it? Will it provide good will? Is it appropriate in your circumstances? A number of companies refuse to provide it for particular categories of employee. They reason that packers, for example, who spend their working hours mindlessly stuffing products into plastic bags, derive little pleasure and certainly no job satisfaction from what they do each day. Pay them when they are away and they'll soon realise that sitting at home is a lot more pleasant than going to work. By contrast, the same companies will allow sick pay for their office staff and, indeed, for shift managers and supervisors.

ill health and injury

At the other end of the spectrum, many employers make up the difference between SSP and the employee's standard rate of pay as a matter of course – and pay normal wages for the 'waiting days' before SSP takes effect. It would be perfectly reasonable for an employer to decide, say, that any payment on top of SSP will be at the management's discretion. If this is made clear at the outset, the proprietor will have allowed themselves absolute flexibility. There are all sorts of possible variations, however: payment of the difference between SSP and basic wages, after six months' service, for up to a maximum of eight weeks in any one calendar year is another example.

SSP can never be a bonus. Employers are not permitted to pay full wages *and* hand over SSP to the employee – even if they were silly enough to want to provide what would amount to a reward for absence. The most the employer can hand out is normal pay minus the SSP due, and then use the SSP to top it up to the original gross level.

Given the numerous possibilities for company sick pay, what is essential from the employer's viewpoint is that:

- the minimum length of service requirement is stated;
- the way of calculating any sick pay is defined;
- the maximum length of the period of entitlement is stated;
- the 'sickness year' is accurately described;
- if appropriate, it is unequivocally stated that there is no entitlement to company sick pay.

Statutory Sick Pay

Since April 1994, the total responsibility for SSP payments falls on employers. However, you may qualify for a refund (at the time of writing, if what you have paid out in SSP is equal to, or in excess of, 13 per cent of the total NI contributions – check the current position with your local DSS office). Under Small Employers' Relief, you

ill health and injury

can recover 100 per cent of the amount paid, but not for the first four weeks of an employee's 'period of incapacity for work' (see page 00). This four-week 'entitlement threshold' can be calculated as *either* four times the weekly rate of SSP or four times the number of qualifying days in the week.

You recover this money by deducting it from the NI contributions submitted monthly or quarterly to the Inland Revenue.

This is a fairly complicated area. If you need to examine it in any detail, the DSS has a number of useful publications you can get from your local DSS office. What follows here is a general description of the scheme, with particular emphasis on some of the more common pitfalls.

Waiting days

No employee is entitled to SSP during the first three days of the sickness that caused their absence from work, unless there is a previous, linked period of absence. These so-called *waiting days* do not have to be working days.

Linking

Periods of incapacity for work (PIW) can be linked. Any number of PIWs can be linked, provided that each PIW extends for at least four days, and each occurred within eight weeks of the preceding one. PIW days include all days, both weekend and working.

Linking has two effects. First, waiting days are only required in the first spell of illness. Second, the employee will exhaust their entitlement to SSP sooner than if there had been no linking – because linking produces what looks like a continuous period of sickness.

It isn't at all clear whether linking is only possible when applied strictly to a continuation of the same illness or condition that kept the employee away from work in the first place. Some conditions may manifest themselves in a variety of

ill health and injury

different symptoms – but all with the same root cause. As the employer, your task is not, however, to make medical judgements: doctors themselves have difficulty in this area.

Entitlement

Broadly speaking, an employee's entitlement to SSP is limited to 28 weeks for any single or linked period of incapacity in a year. If there is no linking, the 28 week period starts again.

Exclusions

Employees have *no* right to SSP if, on the first day of their period of incapacity for work:

- they are over State pension age (65 for both men and women) or are under 16;
- they have not done at least one day's work for you (in the case of new employees);
- their earnings are below the earnings limit (£64 per week at the time of writing, but check the current position);
- they are in legal custody or serving a term of imprisonment.

Employees do not qualify for SSP if they produce a medical certificate for someone else – even if that someone else is their child or dependant. There are a few other more technical reasons for exclusion, which your local DSS office will inform you of, should you need to know.

Proof of illness

Employees have a duty to notify their employers of absence. For the first seven days of absence, all that SSP usually requires is that the employee complete a self-certification note or form – either the DSS form SC2, or the employer's version thereof. Thereafter, a doctor's or hospital certificate will always be needed.
What the employer *cannot* require is:

- notification any earlier than before the end of the first qualifying day;
- a doctor's certificate or completion of some sort of printed form in the initial seven days;
- continuing notification more frequently than at seven-day intervals.

This is an account of what the employer cannot do in relation to SSP requirements. However, some employers may for their own purposes have stricter rules, in relation to timing for example, when the employee's presence or absence is critical (an airline pilot, to take an extreme example).

REPEATED ABSENCE AND LONG-TERM SICKNESS

There is a point at which any employee's continuing absence or repeated absences may start to harm your business. You *may* wish to retain the employee, but perhaps your business cannot afford it. In these circumstances, you may be driven to look very closely at what is called the employee's capability to carry out their part of the contract.

Your options for action depend on how long the employee has been in your service. If they have had less than two years' service with you, it is possible to dismiss them without having to give a reason for doing so. If, however, they have had more than two years' service with you, you will have to behave much more reasonably and properly if you are to avoid a claim of unfair dismissal.

There are some commonly mistaken beliefs about when it is possible to dismiss an employee, and when it is not. For example, contrary to much opinion, you can in fact fire someone despite the fact that they have sent in a medical certificate; you can also dismiss someone before their entitlement to sick leave has expired. However, the vast majority of employers will not want to dump people simply because it is justifiable legally, but will want to act carefully and reasonably. The checklist below sets out what you ought to do and relates to intermittent as well as longer-term sickness.

ill health and injury

The advantages of using the checklist below are two-fold: first, you will be showing yourself to be a thoughtful and fair employer; second, you will have guarded yourself against any claim for unfair dismissal which might be made by a longer-serving employee.

SICKNESS CHECKLIST

- Talk to the employee: explain why their absences are creating a serious problem.
- Investigate the facts – openly
- Take medical advice, if you can, when necessary (the section that follows goes into the law on this subject)
- Tell the employee what timing you think is reasonable in the situation – e.g. how long before the next event, which might be a return to work, or a decision to dismiss, or something in between
- If there is sporadic but repeated absence, tell the employee what you are likely to do if the pattern persists
- Consider alternatives. Is there another job, or lighter work, which might help?

If you want access to medical information from the employee's doctor, you'll be subject to the Access to Medical Reports Act, 1988. The procedure is not as complicated as it sounds. As an employer you have got to do two important things first:

- Tell the employee, in writing, what you want to do
- Tell the employee that they have certain rights.

The rights of the employee

The employee has the right simply to refuse to permit access to their medical records. Thereafter you will have no choice but to proceed without the benefit of any information in the records. The employee's refusal will not necessarily weigh against

them – they may be doing no more than insisting on their right to privacy.
The employee has other rights as well. Let's presume that the employee has consented in principle to the application to their doctor. This employee is entitled to insist that the report be sent to them first, i.e. before you have a chance to see it. If the employee makes such a choice, it is your duty to inform the doctor of this fact, *in writing*.

If the employee doesn't like or doesn't agree with what the doctor has said, they may request amendments. The doctor may or may not agree. Whatever the doctor decides, the employee retains the right, finally, to withhold consent to the report being sent to the employer, in any form.

Beneath the surface of this procedure there may be a dilemma of ethics that can affect the doctor and, indirectly, yourself, as the employer. The doctor may decide that it would be harmful to the patient if they were to be told of their actual condition. The doctor may also feel that revealing this condition to you, the employer, would amount to a breach of ethics. It's a delicate area. You cannot force the hand of either your employee or their doctor; you can only act upon the information provided.

The checklist opposite mentions the need to tell the employee when you intend to take action – and what form such action might take. It is very important to understand that sickness *is not a disciplinary offence*. Anything said to the employee about their sickness record cannot be construed as a warning. This is not an exercise in semantics: it's a vital differentiation.

Repeated absence
This is an area fraught with difficulties. For one thing, it is impossible to define the moment when absences become absenteeism in individual cases; for another, it is very unwise to single someone out for any sort of action, whether this concerns absence or a disciplinary offence. If you are to be seen as a fair employer, you should not pick out the receptionist and ignore the storekeeper when both are in a similar situation.

ill health and injury

When an individual is repeatedly absent, things may not be as they seem. It's easy enough for an employee to pick up the telephone, call the company and say that they are unwell. The real reason for their absence may be quite different. It may be that someone else is ill – a child, a partner, an ageing relative – or that there is some sort of conflict at home, or that the employee hates coming to work because their supervisor is a bully.

These are all reasons with which an employer may find sympathy; indeed, they may be able to do something to help, given the chance. It is all too easy to forget that, when an employee has been with us for any length of time, we have an investment – what the employee knows and can do is valuable to us, and should not be discarded lightly. So, the checklist's suggestion of investigation – which may be as simple as a sympathetic conversation with the employee – is well worth pursuing.

You will have less sympathy with the employee who is simply playing truant. If you can prove that this is what they are doing, and there have been a number of offences (rather than one isolated instance), you can take disciplinary action, up to and including dismissal (these matters are discussed in more detail in Chapter 7). Before you reach these points, the time you spend in talking to your employees is likely to be well repaid – but remember to listen as well. It will also help you and your employees if you record your discussions in writing, however briefly: a simple statement of what you talked about and how it ended up will be sufficient.

pregnancy and maternity benefits 3

ANTENATAL CARE

Later chapters in this book refer to drunkenness, fighting, stealing, drug abuse – topics we all recognise instantly as problem areas. So why a chapter on pregnancy and the workplace? There is a single, compelling reason: it is a complex area, and it's very easy to get things wrong. Since pregnancy is more commonly encountered than any of the cases mentioned in that first sentence, this chapter deals with what is usual before proceeding to the uncommon.

Every pregnant employee is entitled to time off for antenatal care – and to be paid for that time (this applies to expectant mothers only – expectant fathers have no entitlement to time off). There used to be exclusions (related to length of service, for example), but these have disappeared, and this is now a general right. The effect of this is that even an employee who told you, on the very first day she started work with you, that she is pregnant is entitled to this benefit. As her employer, you must pay her during her authorised absences; there is no means of recovering this money from the State.

However, it isn't enough for the employee merely to say that she is pregnant. Her employer is entitled to ask her to produce proof. This proof can be provided by one of the following individuals only:

- a registered medical practitioner
- a registered midwife
- a registered health visitor.

In practice, it is likely that the employee will inform you verbally that, on the advice of one or another of the above, her first appointment at the antenatal clinic has been booked – and ask for time off to attend. It would be unreasonable to expect written

pregnancy and maternity benefits

evidence at this point; nor does the law expect it. However, for subsequent visits you may, at your discretion, ask to see:

- a certificate, signed by any of the three professionals mentioned on the previous page, confirming that the employee is pregnant;
- the employee's appointment card, or some other document, verifying the time and date of her intended visit.

If you have given the employee reasonable notice that you want to see these documents, and she fails to provide them, you are not required to give paid time off. But she is not compelled to produce them unless you have asked for them specifically.

Frequency of antenatal check-ups

The amount of paid time off an employee is entitled to is not clearly stated in the law, which speaks of 'reasonable amounts'. The law gives no guidance as to what is or is not reasonable, but it is a little easier to establish the norm. Using this, what may be expected is that:

- check-ups will start between the eighth and twelfth week of pregnancy;
- the intervals between check-ups will be approximately one month;
- in the sixth and seventh months, visits are likely to be fortnightly;
- in the final month, they'll be weekly.

What if an employee apparently needs to have more frequent visits than this? What is or is not reasonable in that situation? Again, there is no clear guide. There have been relatively few occasions on which an employer has been taken to court for refusing to grant paid time off. When this has happened, however, the employer has tended to lose whenever the increased frequency stemmed from medical advice. In other words, if the doctor says it is necessary, you, as the employer, have to accept their opinion.

Timing of antenatal visits

If you've got a pregnant part-time employee who works mornings only, can you not ask her to make appointments in the afternoons? The position is that you can ask – but you can't require. It may be impossible for her to arrange – because the clinic only functions in the morning, or because she has other things to do in the afternoons. You have no right to insist.

Nor can you demand that she make up the time in any way. You are not permitted to rearrange the normal pattern of her working hours so that visits just happen to coincide with her time off. As to the amount of time she is allowed for each visit, a number of test cases have established that travelling and waiting time are included. Medical appointment systems leave a lot to be desired: delays are not uncommon.

There are no rights relating to infertility treatment until it succeeds and the employee becomes pregnant.

Paying for antenatal visits

Current legislation intends that the employee shall neither suffer nor gain from absence for antenatal care. Provided the employee has been given permission for her absence (she cannot merely presume permission), she will be entitled to a pro-rata payment for the time involved. To calculate this, take an average week's pay and divide it by the normal hours worked – there is no upper limit. If the employee works variable hours from week to week, take the last twelve weeks and work out an average. Once you've arrived at a mean hourly rate, apply it to the time spent away from work.

Remember that the employee is not intended to make a profit. Say, for example, one of your employees, whose normal working hours were 9am to 1pm, left the place of work at 11am but did not finish at the clinic until 2pm – your responsibility is to pay her until 1pm only.

pregnancy and maternity benefits

MATERNITY LEAVE

Since October 1994, the rules concerning the right to maternity leave are as follows:

- There is a general right to fourteen weeks' maternity leave for all pregnant employees, regardless of how long they have been in your service. This period of maternity leave can start up to eleven weeks before the expected week of childbirth
- Employees with at least two years' continuous service are entitled to extended maternity leave, in addition to the fourteen-week period. This right is to take time off up to the twenty-ninth week after the birth. But some part-timers will be automatically excluded if they work for less than eight hours per week, or have been with you for less than five years working between eight and sixteen hours per week.

Right to return

An employee is entitled to return to 'exactly the same job, on exactly the same terms and conditions, as though she had not been absent'. For very small companies and organisations this requirement may be extremely onerous. If a small employer has five employees or fewer (including the woman seeking to return), they can legally avoid any claim of unfair dismissal if it is impossible or impracticable to reinstate the employee. There is an exception to this exception, but it relates only to teachers in small state-aided schools.

'The same job'

Employers are allowed some latitude here. A secretary may be asked to work for someone else when she comes back. Elsewhere, an employee may be required to work a different shift. What is necessary is that the character of the work, its location and relative seniority, should be preserved.

pregnancy and maternity benefits

A returning employee has no right, under the maternity provisions, to require the employer to grant reduced hours or different hours – but she may have a right under the sex discrimination legislation. Before you dismiss her request, think what you might arrange for a man with the same need, albeit for a different reason.

'As though she had not been absent'
Your employee is entitled to expect that her service will be regarded as continuous throughout the period of her absence. She should therefore benefit from any pay increases there may have been in the interim. If there is a pension scheme, her membership must be continuous. Conversely, if there has been a general worsening of pay and conditions, she must bear this too.

There are unlikely to be that many company cars around in smaller organisations: however, if a pregnant employee has one, you will first have to ask yourself what the contractual arrangement was. Did you have the foresight, originally, to require that the company car be returned at any time, on demand, when you issued it for her use? If you didn't, you're in a grey area. The line of least resistance suggests that you let her keep it for the moment. But, if the business is on hard times and you cannot afford to buy or hire another one for whoever is to do her job while she is away, maybe you have no real choice.

Failure to reinstate

A failure to reinstate an employee to her old job after maternity leave immediately leads to a presumption of redundancy. The cost of redundancy for a long-service employee may be considerable, and you may also have to face up to a claim that the woman concerned was unfairly selected (redundancy and selection are dealt with in more detail in Chapter 8). It's up to you to prove that, whatever your reason, failure to reinstate did not involve redundancy. At the same time, you must prove that your reason was not directly or indirectly concerned with the employee's pregnancy – dismissal as the result of pregnancy is automatically unfair.

pregnancy and maternity benefits

It is very rare for employers to succeed in justifying dismissal (as opposed to fairly selected redundancy) during pregnancy or the following months. Since October 1994 the law is even stricter than it was. Take the example of a woman who is breast-feeding and who might therefore justifiably be ruled out of carrying on her work in a factory-type environment. Her employer is first bound to offer alternative work, even if this is of a different nature and perhaps less well rewarded. If no such work can be found, the employee must be suspended from work on the grounds of maternity, until she is again available for work. During this period of suspension she will be entitled to her normal pay. An employee is not, however, entitled to suspension with pay if she has turned down an employer's offer of alternative work.

STATUTORY MATERNITY PAY

As the employer, you hand out Statutory Maternity Pay (SMP) and recover it from National Insurance contributions – provided you've stuck to the rules. There is no connection between SMP and a woman's right to maternity leave.

There are two rates at which SMP is paid. These are known as the *higher rate* and the *lower rate*. All women who have been continuously employed, whether part time or full time, in the same job for 26 weeks are entitled to SMP at the higher rate (90 per cent of actual earnings) for the first six weeks of maternity leave, followed by up to twelve weeks at the standard rate (now raised to parity with the higher rate of SSP). To qualify, the woman's weekly earnings must be above the lower earnings limit for NI contributions, and the woman must still be employed within the qualifying week.

Some technical terms

The expected week of childbirth (EWC) is the week during which the birth is expected. The qualifying week (QW) is the fifteenth week before the EWC. In either case, a week is seven days, starting on a Sunday and ending on the following Saturday.

pregnancy and maternity benefits

In order to qualify for SMP, the employee must have at least 26 weeks' continuous service with you and she must still be employed by you during at least part of the QW. When you are checking this, remember that weeks run from Sunday to Saturday: your working pattern, if different, is irrelevant.

A tiny number of employers spend a great deal of time trying to find ways in which they can avoid, or in this case evade, liability in almost any area of maternity benefit. Some of them worked out that, by dismissing an employee before she qualified for SMP, they'd avoid what they saw as an administrative nuisance and an initial cash outflow. As long as the employee concerned has been employed by them, continuously, for at least eight weeks, this won't work. If it can be shown that the dismissal was made for this reason, the employee will be deemed to have been employed until the QW.

For special cases, you should check with your local DSS office: such cases include agency workers, seasonal workers, regular casual workers and situations in which there is a premature or earlier than expected birth, a miscarriage or a stillborn child.

The employer's responsibilities

You need to be able to work out when your liability begins, since you, the employer, are responsible for handing out SMP. Your employee is required to give you 21 days' notice of the start of her maternity leave, which you can ask for in writing. Strictly speaking, a failure to provide notice will disqualify her from SMP, but the law speaks of what is 'reasonably practicable'. If the employee doesn't agree with an unfavourable decision, she can appeal to a Department of Social Security Adjudication Officer.

Your employee will also need a medical certificate stating the EWC at this time. She also has a duty to report to you any change of circumstances that may affect her right to SMP. If she were to work for another employer after her child is born, for example, the first employer's liability ceases. It also ends if she is taken into police custody, and SMP is not payable during any week that the employee is outside the European

pregnancy and maternity benefits

Union. There is also a strict rule that an employee cannot receive SMP and SSP at the same time.

The need for record keeping

Because you are entitled to recover SMP amounts from NI deductions, the State requires an 'accounting' (something that may be checked, for example an extract from your pay records). Many small businesses use an external accountant to handle pay calculations and record keeping, who will know what needs to be done. If you don't use an external accountant, there are proprietary do-it-yourself pay systems that meet the requirements.

As a general rule, you must keep records, including medical evidence, for at least three years after the end of the relevant tax year. You must not overlook this need. It's a criminal offence to fail to keep these records. A DSS inspector can enter your premises at any reasonable time, and there are penalties if you do not comply with reasonable requests. There's also a substantial fine plus repeats per offence in prospect for non-compliance. It's worth taking a bit of trouble.

MATERNITY ALLOWANCE

If an employee is not entitled to SMP, she *may* qualify for the Maternity Allowance. As her employer, your task is to advise her to apply for the second, if she does not qualify for the first.

You are required to fill in and give to your employee a DSS form, SMP1, stating why you believe that SMP does not apply. At the same time, you should hand back the medical certificate that predicts the week of childbirth. Armed with these two documents, the employee can talk to the local DSS office.

This benefit is payable for up to eighteen weeks, beginning at the eleventh week before the expected date of childbirth. If your employee chooses to work beyond this

pregnancy and maternity benefits

eleventh week, the period of benefit will not be extended: she reduces her entitlement to MA by working on. She cannot be paid either SMP or Maternity Allowance while she is still working.

Maternity Allowance is paid out by the State rather than the employer and is not subject to deductions for tax or NI. The prime qualification for employees is that they have paid suitable NI contributions for at least six months of the preceding 66 months. The local DSS office will explain the precise requirement.

4 holidays and time off

HOLIDAYS

Employees have no statutory right to holidays – even bank holidays – but, as an average small employer, you are likely to have recognised the need for your employees to have some occasional, paid respite from the treadmill.

Making the terms clear

As with all other areas, it pays to be specific. Assume that you have declared that paid leave for all employees amounts to, say, 20 days per annum, plus bank holidays. Sadly, this isn't precise enough. Imagine for a moment some of the questions a new employee might have:

- How does it work? Do I have to wait a year before I get a holiday?
- Or is there some sort of accrual system?
- Can I take more holiday than I have strictly accrued? (I started in May. There's no chance of a fortnight's holiday in August otherwise, and I've booked it.)
- Does this 'per annum' mean January to December?
- Can I take it all at once? I've been wanting to visit my son in Canada for ages.
- If I don't use it all this year, can I carry the unused bit forward?

The longer-serving employee may have a few questions, too, and they will have had time to develop more esoteric queries:

- My job means I always get Mondays off. When it's a bank holiday Monday you pay other people for it. Shouldn't you pay me too?
- I was taken ill on the Friday night. I spent the whole fortnight in bed. Can I take my proper holiday later?

36

holidays and time off

Explaining the 'leave year' and calculating entitlement

Beneath these innocent questions lurks a potential source of nuisance, sometimes a cost, that you can avoid. For example, you will have stated the number of paid leave days, plus bank holidays, but you won't have explained the leave year. In practice, you are likely to use the calendar year, but there's no reason why you shouldn't have your leave year run from, say, 1 April of one year to 31 March of the next if you choose.

So far as the employee's first year of service is concerned, you should usually say something about holidays in the letter in which you offer them the job. For example:

> Holidays will accrue pro rata with length of service during your first twelve months with the company.

If the year's allowance is 20 days, then each month of completed service will attract a 'credit' of 1.6 days. After three months the employee will have earned 4.9 days: no doubt you'll be gracious enough to concede five days in the event.

But what if your employee asks for ten days at this point? You'd be within your rights to refuse to allow this, unless you had agreed to it before they joined. However, you *could* concede the additional days without pay, or you could permit the employee to 'anticipate accrual' and grant the extra five days with pay.

Following this last option means you will have done a deal with the employee. This is a contract in its own right. If the employee then leaves you, two months later, you'll be out of pocket. You might be tempted to deduct this from the final pay cheque – which appears the simplest solution – but in fact you have no right to do so. If you think back to the contract of employment, you will see that all you have got is a right to sue for recovery in a civil court – nothing more. Unless the employee consents to the deduction, you are stuck. In fact, even when the employee agrees to the deduction in advance, you might not be able to enforce it if the employee withdraws consent at the last minute.

holidays and time off

Carrying holiday entitlement over, and other issues

If an employee is hard pressed at the year-end and would have difficulty taking their holiday entitlement without jeopardising what they are working on, you may well decide to allow them to carry holidays forward to the next. You would be best advised, however, to make clear at the outset that 'carry-over' is not normally an option. If need be, you can always make exceptions, and it is better that the choice should be yours. If you don't make this clear, an employee could build up a six-week credit (for example) and demand the time off, all in one go – which might lead to difficulties.

Holidays and sickness

A different type of problem is presented by the employee who overstays an agreed extended holiday abroad and arrives back, two weeks or so late, with a medical certificate, apparently from a foreign doctor. This will be discussed in a later chapter.

More commonly, an employee's fortnight's holiday may be wrecked by a bout of sickness that keeps them at home. Unless there's a prior agreement, it's up to you to decide whether to classify this period as holiday or sick leave. If the employee qualifies for SSP, it can be paid in the normal way: even bank holidays can be used as waiting days. But there is no rule: it is down to the individual employer's discretion.

Bank holidays

Bank holidays can be another source of friction. What about the part-time employee who does not work on Mondays and who thinks they should be paid for bank holiday Mondays, because the other employees are? Unfortunately (from the employee's point of view), an employee is entitled to be paid only for those bank holidays that fall within their normal working pattern – so this particular employee would be entitled to be paid for Good Friday, but not Easter Monday.

There is one final point about holidays that employers often overlook: holidays continue to accrue to employees who are kept on the books, even when they have used up any entitlement to company sick pay. In such circumstances, holidays are likely to mean paid bank holidays as well as paid holidays.

OTHER ABSENCES

Jury service

Men and women between 18 and 70 (normally 65) may be required for jury service unless they are exempt because of either their profession (for example, police officers, those in the legal profession) or their status (for example, peers and lunatics). You have to release an employee who is summoned for jury service. If the temporary loss of that employee is going to be particularly damaging to your business, you can write to the Lord Chancellor's department and plead that point. Should the Lord Chancellor's staff feel that the most that is going to be caused by the employee's absence is inconvenience, then they will not grant the request – but they are receptive to genuine cases.

You must release an employee for jury service, but you are not bound to pay them during their absence for this purpose. If you do not, the juror can claim a Financial Loss Allowance from the court. It isn't very generous, as you might expect, and many employers either make up the difference between this and average pay or pay as normal, of course.

Court appearances

If an employee is required to attend as a witness or as the accused in a criminal court – or as witness, plaintiff or defendant in a civil one – most employers take the view that they should be allowed to go. If you don't release the employee, the court can issue an order demanding their presence.

As with jury service, you are not bound to pay the employee during absence for this purpose.

Medical appointments

If an employee wants to take time off to see their doctor, optician, osteopath and so on, their absence should be treated just like any other absence – they have no entitlement to be paid for these visits and, even if there is a company sick pay

holidays and time off

scheme, such visits are very often excluded. You are not being unreasonable if you remind employees that most GPs run a morning and an evening surgery and they should try to visit them then – emergencies, of course, are a different matter altogether.

It is better, here as elsewhere, to have one fixed position. If the company's rule is that there will be no payment for absence, for whatever reason, there's no room for argument. When payment is discretionary, it isn't always easy to be consistent, and consistency is the hallmark of a good and fair boss.

Other people's illnesses

When a partner or a child is ill and needs to be looked after, your employee has no right to SSP. It is also unlikely that they will have any right to payment from your company sick pay scheme. Most of these absences happen as the result of an emergency: a child develops measles, an ageing mother falls and breaks her hip. By their nature they will tend to be initially unauthorised: nobody plans these things.

There is a strong, moral argument in favour of being sympathetic to your employee's problems and helping them when you can. But there's a pragmatic argument as well: if you are not sympathetic, you will encourage your employee to try to disguise the real causes of their absence. That won't help you, or the employee, in the longer term.

Public office

The law says that Justices of the Peace (JPs) and members of local councils, for example, must be allowed a reasonable amount of time off during working hours to carry out their public duties. An employee who believes that they are not being given reasonable time off can complain to an industrial tribunal.

As usual, the law does not define what is or is not reasonable. It implies that reasonableness will depend on circumstances, and that employer and employee must try to agree whenever possible. You may argue that the extent of the employee's

holidays and time off

absences, or their absence at a particular time, is highly damaging to the business. If the employee disagrees, the tribunal must decide.

'During working hours' is a key phrase. You are not permitted to force the employee to make up the time lost, by working additional hours. However, once again, you are not required by law to pay for time off for these purposes.

The list of offices falling within this law includes not only JPs and council members, but also members of NHS Trusts, water authorities, boards of grant-maintained schools and others. If you are in any doubt, telephone the nearest ACAS office (see Useful Addresses, p. 86).

Territorial Army and Special Constables

Members of the Territorial Army and the Special Constabulary are volunteers, so there are no concessions for employees wanting to take time off for activities in these areas. Most employers will expect the employees concerned to use their annual leave for summer camps and extended weekend training periods, although some employers may allow additional paid or unpaid leave. It's for you to decide.

Religious festivals of other faiths

Some of our public holidays (Christmas Day and Good Friday, for example) are centred on Christian festivals. What happens when an employee of a different faith asks for time off to observe a religious custom, practice or occasion which they consider important? Under the Race Relations Code of Practice, an employee has no *statutory* right to time off for these purposes, but employers are asked to do what they can to accommodate needs of this sort.

Looking for another job

If an employee has been with you for more than two years, and you have made their job redundant, you are bound to allow them reasonable paid time off, during working hours, to look for a new job or arrange some form of training as an

holidays and time off

alternative – provided they are under formal notice. This time off need not invariably be for the purpose of job interviews. Employees may need time to go to local employment agencies, the Job Centre, etc.

If you do not permit this, the employee can appeal to an industrial tribunal. If the tribunal's decision goes against you, it can cost you up to 40 per cent of the employee's pay for the entire period of notice.

Trade union and safety representatives

Trade union legislation provides for statutory time off with pay for union officials who are performing specific duties. Trade union members are less well provided for, although shop stewards may qualify in certain circumstances.

There is an ACAS *Code of Practice on Time Off for Trade Union Duties and Activities* – a bit of a mouthful, but worth getting from your local ACAS office. Safety representatives, appointed by an independent union, may qualify for paid time off, for example to attend training courses. To help you here, there's a Health and Safety Commission Code of Practice: in combination with the ACAS code mentioned above, it will provide most of the answers to your questions.

discipline – the groundwork 5

KEEPING IT FORMAL

The strongest argument in favour of formal systems when it comes to discipline is that the informal ones don't work. The difficulty is that the average small employer *must* concentrate on the business and has precious little time available to do much beyond the bare essentials.

You should be reassured to learn that nobody important expects small businesses to have refined, sophisticated systems. A quick look at the way in which industrial tribunals function will demonstrate this. They do not require or demand of small businesses a mass of written rules and procedures. By contrast, they may occasionally be critical of large companies that have the resources to install and run suitable systems, but have failed to do so.

The first chapter of this book suggested the use of just three pre-printed forms. One of these is the *Employer's Rules and Procedures* (sometimes called the Disciplinary Code – see pp. 14–15), which is based on the ACAS Code of Practice. It's a very useful form to have, in terms of minimum protection for employees and employers alike. The form lists three categories of conduct that you, the employer, will find unwelcome:

- minor offences and unsatisfactory conduct
- serious offences or misconduct
- gross misconduct.

The form also gives examples within each heading, which is particularly useful, as the employee is not required to make subtle differentiations between classifications. The examples speak for themselves. Persistent lateness, for instance, is quoted at one end of the spectrum and wilful destruction of the employer's property at the other.

discipline – the groundwork

You should not, however, rely on this form exclusively. Your first line of defence – and, probably, that of your employees, too – lies not in this single document but in the combination of all three that have been recommended. They depend upon each other.

The rules and procedures that appear in the suggested version are not intended to be comprehensive. You are at liberty to insist on additional rules, provided that they are sensible and reasonable.

LOCAL RULES

It is worth starting with a few examples. A small injection-moulding company operates occasional night shifts when business is good. At night the internal door to the packaging materials store is left unlocked because there's a fire exit through there. The local rule might say:

> Except in the event of fire or some other similar emergency, no employee may enter the packaging store during a night shift other than when accompanied by the shift supervisor.

This rule was put in place – but only after an accident had occurred: a case of being wise after the event. An employee, on night shift, ran short of cartons. He went to the store and, while he was pulling some carton flats from the top of an unstable stack, something like a ton and a half of pallets and packaging materials fell on him. His injuries were very severe, and his absence was not noticed for almost an hour.

Take another far less serious but still important example:

> If you ring up an incorrect amount on the till, tell your manager what happened at the earliest opportunity.

discipline – the groundwork

This sort of rule is likely to be appropriate when there's a newish junior employee, but it's your responsibility to balance the till roll with the cash each evening.

There's a great difference of degree between these two examples. The first is (literally) a matter of life or death; by contrast, the second is hardly life threatening. You'd be well advised to commit the first rule to writing and make sure that the employees concerned read it. To be absolutely safe, you'd ask them to sign it to say that they *had* read it. Even then, you'd put up a very large sign over the door to the store, incorporating this rule. It's that important.

In the second case, a verbal instruction would be enough. If the employee forgets on one occasion, the consequences are unlikely to be tragic. You would probably remind the employee and ask them not to do it again.

These examples imply two underlying principles so far as local rules are concerned:

- Your rules can relate to health and safety, methods of working, behaviour, dress (within reasonable limits), security – anything that is significant within your business and your location
- Ideally you'd commit them all to writing, but verbal instructions and custom and practice can be perfectly adequate. You will need to decide whether one or two of the rules are so important that you must write them down, or display them conspicuously.

Ensuring all employees understand your rules

Writing your local rules down, or displaying them, sounds easy enough, but remember that not all your employees will have English as their first language. In order to prevent, for example, computers being 'helpfully' switched off at the power supply in the evening, with disastrous results, make sure your warning notices are written so that *all* your employees will understand.

MANAGEMENT'S ROLE IN DISCIPLINE

It's a lot easier to be a manager in a large organisation than in a small one. The big-company manager can often pass the buck to one or other of the in-house experts when things go wrong. There are almost always formal rules and procedures. And there is a much more impersonal style and atmosphere.

Contrast these elements with what goes on in a small business. There are no experts, little is written down, and the atmosphere is intensely personal. You will know the employees who have been with you for any length of time very well. In addition, you'll probably know their partners, some of their children and a great deal about their personal circumstances. Whether you like it or not, you are involved. Inevitably there are times when this does not make the manager's task easy.

Testing your response

Managers are supposed to act in a fair and reasonable way, but it doesn't always work that way. If you have taken some fairly rigorous form of disciplinary action and you have a vague, nagging feeling that you might have gone too far, a useful test is to ask yourself this: 'If, tomorrow, I speak to an absolutely impartial outsider – someone who has no connection with my business – would they think that what I did today amounted to a completely fair, balanced and *proportionate* response to what happened?'

Quite often, when you apply this test (which, incidentally, is similar to tests used by industrial tribunals most of the time), you'll find that your self-doubt was well founded. So, if you are contemplating anything dramatic, don't do it today. Go home and think about it overnight.

Discipline may not be a word at the forefront of your mind, as a manager. Instead you might think in terms of phrases like 'poor timekeeping' or, perhaps, 'unauthorised absence from time to time'. But, if you've formulated reasonable rules, it's up to you to insist that they are kept. A simple example will illustrate this. Your

discipline – the groundwork

business opens its doors at 8am. Florence asks if you'd mind if she came in at 8.30 tomorrow, exceptionally, as her husband, who normally takes the kids to school, is having to take his car to be repaired. You are likely to allow this, but what happens if the same thing happens next week? What if, after a while, and because you are always so accommodating, she no longer bothers to ask? And what if this practice becomes habitual...? If it goes on for any length of time and becomes customary, you may be judged to have created, by default if not collusion, a new set of working hours for Florence. Her working day now begins at 8.30 – which might not enchant her colleagues. If she can do this, why can't everybody else?

Early informal action is a lot better than later, heavy-handed intervention, even if this is sometimes easier said than done in a small, relaxed organisation. There's no doubt, however, that the manager who is too friendly, who wants to be one of the boys or girls, is likely to be storing up future problems. At the other end of the scale, managers whose styles are modelled on Vlad the Impaler or Catherine the Great are just as bad.

Reducing the likelihood of disciplinary problems

One way of avoiding problems of this kind involves the much-used phrases 'motivation' and 'job satisfaction'.

Job satisfaction is notoriously difficult to define. Bearing in mind that you must be your own personnel manager from time to time, consider this question, which is quite often put to young hopefuls in this discipline. Which of the following statements is likely to be correct?

a) Job satisfaction leads to good performance.
b) Good performance leads to job satisfaction.

Most people plump for (a) – and get it wrong. A number of people who enjoy what they are doing enormously are, sadly, not much good at it. So there's no guarantee that their self-satisfaction, their job satisfaction, will profit the employer at all.

discipline – the groundwork

The second statement makes more sense. Most of us do not go to work just for the money – we want more than that. Among other things we want some respect for what we do and how we do it. We want recognition and occasional praise. A constant diet of criticism, or merely being taken for granted, will slowly but surely destroy our self-esteem. When this happens, we will work less hard, less well, and grudgingly. Going to work each day will become a chore rather than something to which we look forward.

In a well-run and capably managed business, any employee will expect criticism from time to time – but they will expect this criticism to be tempered by occasional praise. At any level, no matter how ordinary the job, it is always possible to find something complimentary to say about what the employee has done. And it's important that you should do so. Employees need the esteem of their boss and their colleagues – it's a vital ingredient, and without it there will be no job satisfaction.

Young employees are vulnerable; they are also malleable. They will be particularly susceptible to praise or criticism and they will be easily influenced by your existing employees. Here, the small organisation may have a considerable advantage over a big one: you can manage the young employee's exposure to the influence of other staff members. If they have to work at some time with the one 'old lag' in your company, make it later rather than sooner.

DISCIPLINARY REMEDIES

Everything written about disciplinary procedures seems always to be heavily laced with words like 'fair', 'even-handed', 'reasonable', 'without fear or favour', 'proportionate' and so on. The words in question are significant. Unwary employers sometimes find out *how* meaningful they are only when they arrive in front of an industrial tribunal. The rest of this chapter is devoted to the practical application of the principles that are implied.

discipline – the groundwork

Is it worth doing anything about it?

The answer to this question depends on the circumstances. The fact that you are asking it at all would indicate that the employee hasn't set fire to the building or beaten up their supervisor. So, whatever the infringement, it is minor.

From this starting point you can construct your own checklist. This might amount to:

- Has it happened before? If so, rarely, or often?
- What did you do about it?
- Have other people done it? What was your response then?
- Even if *you* don't much mind, will it annoy or upset other employees?
- Is there a company rule involved? Is this rule normally enforced?
- Is this behaviour undermining your authority?
- How likely is it to happen again?

On the assumption that you have decided that you ought to do something, there are four basic alternatives for action which form a rising scale of seriousness: informal warnings; formal warnings; final warnings; suspension. The next sections look at these in turn.

Informal warnings

Supervisors and managers will issue one or two minor, 'on-the-job' warnings in the course of their everyday work – probably without thinking that what they are doing amounts to a warning at all. It is part of a day's work to tell Beth quietly that she must pay more attention to what she is doing because she is failing to notice sub-standard work that will cause problems later. Explaining to Joe that, when a customer is waiting to be served, it is discourteous to continue his unimportant conversation with another member of staff, is another example. You would only consider moving to the point of a properly conducted informal warning if an employee does, or fails to do, things of this nature repeatedly.

discipline – the groundwork

The examples on the previous page are informal – they were never meant to be part of a formal disciplinary process. As such, you couldn't use them in evidence later because you did not tell either of the employees at the time that these oral warnings were in fact formal and would be recorded as part of your disciplinary procedure. It's important to remember that oral warnings can be informal or formal. It's up to you to decide which – and to say so very clearly if the latter is the case.

There may be many reasons for your decision to administer an informal warning. These may centre, for example, on persistent lateness, absences, sub-standard work, removing guards from machines – anything that you consider would be best nipped in the bud rather than allowed to continue without your commenting on it. At this point, it ought to occur to you that, while your well-intentioned attempt to sort out the problem may work, there is at least a possibility that it may not. So, keep some sort of record of whatever you do. It doesn't have to be elaborate – a note of the time and date when you talked to the person concerned and a brief note of the subject is likely to be adequate.

Delivering an informal warning in a meeting

The circumstances of your meeting are important. The meeting must be private, and you ought to ensure that you are not interrupted. Warnings issued in front of other employees are generally counter-productive. The employee concerned will resent being hauled over the coals in front of their colleagues and may react badly to save face. It is also unlikely that they will take the time and trouble to listen to explanations in these circumstances. If they choose to argue, the whole thing will become a mess.

Set aside a time and a place for a meeting, and explain, quietly and firmly, what you want to talk about. Ask the employee for their comments. It's a mistake to launch immediately into your prepared speech. See what the employee has to say first: you may have misunderstood the situation, even if you thought you had the facts at your disposal.

Such interviews, like good speeches, ought to have a beginning, a middle and an end. The beginning consists of your introduction to the subject of the meeting.

discipline – the groundwork

The middle concerns what the employee says, your point of view and some discussion as to what can be done, by both parties, to solve the problem. The end, which we have not touched on yet, is most important. This is the point at which you summarise the outcome of the meeting.

The form that your summary might take is as follows:

- the substance of your complaint, including reference to any available evidence;
- what you both agreed was a reasonable standard for future performance;
- the period over which improvement is going to be measured and judged;
- what will happen if improvement does not take place.

Appropriate behaviour in the meeting

You are likely to get the best results if, throughout this entire process, you behave in a civilised, courteous way. Don't fall into the trap of sprinkling your remarks with swear words, just because it's normal on the shop floor. It will rebound on you. The individual noted normally for the fruitiness of their vocabulary will become suddenly pious at your expense. Nor is there any need to thump the desk, raise your voice or be generally nasty. The fact that you are dealing with the problem, whatever it is, in a serious, carefully polite manner, will register.

In most instances, you will be alone with the employee. When there's a recognised trade union shop steward around, they may attend, at the employee's request (this won't concern most small-business employers). Beyond this, as a general rule, no other person has a right to be present.

Formal warnings

When you decide that the time has come to issue a formal warning, there is one absolute requirement: you must tell the employee that what you are handing out is a formal warning. This sounds like obvious advice, but you may be surprised to learn how often employees tell industrial tribunals that they didn't realise that their boss wasn't just having a bit of a moan at them.

discipline – the groundwork

The trouble is that warnings do not necessarily have to be given in writing. Just as you should make a note of informal warnings, you should at the very least do the same with the formal versions. However, if there's an argument, a written note of a formal warning is unlikely to be enough. The best way around this is to make sure that all formal warnings are issued in writing. One such sample appears below: there's no need for it to be complicated.

> **Formal warning**
> To: David Purbeck
> Date: 20 November 1998
>
> You and I met yesterday to discuss your misconduct in connection with your removal of the safety guard on the guillotine you operate. You were seen to be removing this yesterday at the beginning of your shift. You had received two earlier informal warnings in October and September of this year relating directly to this practice.
>
> Removing the safety guard is highly dangerous. It is against our rules and, as you were told yesterday, any repetition of this practice will place your job here at risk. If your conduct in this regard is satisfactory over the next three months, this notice will be destroyed. Any recurrence will be regarded as very serious indeed.
>
> Colin Jenks
> Managing Director

This sample warning seems to imply that the person it's addressed to, David Purbeck, is someone the company doesn't want to lose. He has been spoken to twice before, but it looks as though the seriousness of what he is doing hasn't registered. This warning is an honest attempt to get him on to the right track.

Note also that, while it underlines the gravity of the offence, the warning holds out hope. It is not threatening dismissal at this stage, and it makes a point of saying that there is a term to the warning it contains. It will not stay on his file for ever. If he behaves properly over the next three months, the slate will be wiped clean.

discipline – the groundwork

An employee's right of appeal

What the memo does not contain is a *right of appeal*. Whether it is appropriate to contain one will depend on the form of organisation. This particular warning suggests that Mr Jenks, the Managing Director, is the owner and proprietor – that there is no one senior to him, to whom the employee could appeal. If Jenks had been merely the manager, and there was someone senior to him, the warning would have added that the employee had the right to appeal to this more senior individual against the decision to issue a warning. It would, of course, be normal to set a time limit to the right of appeal.

Final warnings

All final warnings must be issued in writing. You will find one such example below. It is a stage on in the case of David Purbeck and suggests that he has not mended his ways:

Final warning
To: David Purbeck
Date: 10 January 1999

This records our meeting at 12.30pm today. Your machine was found to be unguarded this morning at 11 am, and you confirmed at our meeting that you had removed it when you started work this morning.

My note to you dated 20 November 1998 contained a formal warning on the subject of guard removal. You are and have been aware that this practice is a very serious and dangerous breach of our company rules. It clearly amounts to misconduct.

I hereby confirm what you have already been told very firmly. Any repetition of this misconduct will make you liable to dismissal without further warning.

Colin Jenks
Managing Director

discipline – the groundwork

The managing director has decided that he is going to lay the law down firmly this time. If this doesn't persuade the employee to comply with a sensible rule, he may indeed fire him.

It is worth thinking a bit about why the managing director is taking this action. He knows that safety guards are considered by most operators to be a bit of a nuisance: they get in the way; they slow things down. The fact that they also save a lot of fingers is conveniently forgotten. The managing director also knows, however, that it is nearly always the employer who gets the blame – and the fine maybe – when the factory inspector arrives and safety guards are not in position. If there is an accident and the employee is injured, the employee's solicitor will usually advise them to sue the employer for failure to provide safe means of working. Even if the employer can prove that the guards do exist, but that the employee removed them, they may still be responsible – this time for a failure to provide adequate supervision.

Despite the reasonably restrained tone, the managing director has not set a term to this warning. This time he has not said that, if the employee does not re-offend within three months, the warning will be removed. In practice, he is likely to know that no industrial tribunal will ever accept that a warning can last indefinitely. It's no good dragging up warnings that were issued three years ago. By the same token, if you have set a term to a warning, that warning cannot be used once the term has expired. The legal term for this is that it is regarded as being 'spent'.

Suspension

The next chapter deals with this subject in some detail. What you need to know here is that suspension without pay can only be used as a punishment if it is written into the employee's terms and conditions of service. An employer will normally suspend an employee, with pay, during a period when they are investigating, gathering facts and so on. It's not a weapon, and you'd be very unwise to see it as such: it has a nasty habit of blowing up in your face.

incompetence and misconduct 6

SUB-STANDARD WORK

When your newly acquired fork-lift truck driver demolishes the doors for the fifth time in his first two weeks, it will be very clear that this is an employee you cannot afford. This is an employee who, to use the technical word, does not possess something called capability. Employment law says that *capability* relates to skill, aptitude, health and any other physical or mental quality. You have a right to expect that the person concerned will possess an inherent capability to do the job. This person clearly hasn't got it: he'll have to go before he demolishes the entire building.

One way of looking at the case of the fork-lift truck driver is to see it as an extreme example of *sub-standard work*. This may lead you to believe that such work is usually easy to detect and define. This is not the case, particularly when it comes to newcomers.

You are entitled to expect an inherent capability; you are *not* entitled to expect that a newly arrived employee will perform at a high standard without training and practice. Sometimes the slow starters, the slow learners, turn into some of the best producers we have.

Dealing with sub-standard work from established employees

It is not just new members of staff who perform sub-standard work, of course: established employees may also do so. And employees who have been with a company for more than two years have acquired the right not to be unfairly dismissed. If their work has fallen below an acceptable standard you are bound to do a lot more than merely hand over a final wage packet and point the way to the door.

To begin with, you need to assure yourself that their work *has* fallen below an acceptable standard. Are you relying on somebody else's opinion? Is the employee aware of the standard required? Have you told them, clearly, what the job demands? We're not always good at telling people what we really mean.

incompetence and misconduct

Imagine yourself before a tribunal, telling them that you fired Sally, who had been with you for three years, because she can't add up. That's ridiculous: you should have found this out in her first week. On the other hand, you'd have a real case if you could show that her work had declined, had become increasingly careless over the last three months and that, in spite of informal and formal warnings, there had been no improvement.

Sales people present a different problem here. If sales have fallen off generally, it is demonstrably unfair to blame one individual. It is much more likely that, if things are really bad, their job will become redundant. Firing them, to avoid a redundancy payment, will rebound on you.

There may be other scenarios. Poor or careless presentation of the company's products by the representative may be difficult to prove, unless you're with them – and you can't be with them all the time. Administrative incompetence, wrongly transcribed orders and so on, may be easier to detect. As with the earlier example, you'd go through the disciplinary cycle up to, if necessary, dismissal.

You ought also to try to find out why the quality of their work has deteriorated. There may be all sorts of reasons – for example, the employee may be distracted by domestic problems.

Sub-standard work or misconduct?

A certain company requires a salesperson to make an average of eight calls per day, which, given the size of the territory and other factors, is a reasonable expectation. However, the employer has reason to believe that the salesperson is cheating; they discover that many of the visits the salesperson has claimed have not been made at all and that, in some cases, they have substituted a telephone call from home instead.

This is not sub-standard work; this is misconduct. If an employee behaves like this, you may feel that the relationship between you has been irretrievably damaged. If, in addition, they had claimed expenses for trips they didn't make, you might well decide that their behaviour amounts to gross misconduct and you might dismiss the person concerned.

While employment law is weighted in favour of the employee, an employer's opinion, objectively and reasonably held, still carries considerable force. In the context of sub-standard work, your view of the standards necessary within your business is what matters. It's your business: you know more about it than anyone else. But you've got to tell your employees what you want.

HEALTH AND HYGIENE PROBLEMS

Alcohol abuse

Three or four of your staff have just got back from the pub, where they've been celebrating a colleague's twenty-first birthday. They are clearly feeling no pain. What do you do? If there is machinery involved, you'll give them a rocket and send them home. At a pinch, you might issue an informal, even a formal, warning if the circumstances demand it, but generally there's an end to it. The result of such action is that you will not be seen to encourage drunkenness. You are producing a response that is proportionate to the offence. Who knows? On rare, special occasions, you might even turn a blind eye.

The employee who goes to the pub every lunch time, knocks back six pints of beer and spends his afternoons in an alcoholic haze is another matter. So too is the employee who arrives in the morning already smelling of alcohol and visits the loo or a storeroom at intervals throughout the day for the nips they need to keep going. Both these employees look as if they have a dependence on alcohol.

If your company rules say that it is forbidden to bring alcohol on to the premises, there's an obvious disciplinary offence in the second case. Alternatively, you may feel that you have a social duty to help the person concerned to get professional help. Beyond this, however, if you discover that, no matter what you do, the problem is intractable, you will be concerned about the employee's capability to do the job required.

If you know and can demonstrate that an employee's efficiency is significantly impaired, you'll still need to go through the process of warnings, time for improvement and so on. The capability argument will depend on circumstances. There is a difference between a machine shop operator who consumes large quantities of alcohol at lunch time and a clerk who does the same. However, in order to remove these circumstantial distinctions, some organisations have company rules that forbid consumption of any alcohol at certain times, even outside working hours.

Personal hygiene

Body odour always seems to attract comment and uneasy laughter more than constructive action. The advertisement for a deodorant that used to include the phrase 'His best friends wouldn't tell him' was remarkably accurate. Male managers are notoriously bad at coping with this sort of situation, whether it concerns a male or a female member of their staff. They'll always try to pass the buck.

You have a right to expect good standards of hygiene from your staff. If you run a business that has any connection with food then, to put it bluntly, the employee involved must either improve immediately, be redeployed to a non-food area, or – if there is no improvement – go through the disciplinary procedure to the point of dismissal. In a non-food business, the problem may be equally acute but for a different reason – the rest of the staff find it offensive.

If you are in a small business, with a handful of staff, there's nowhere to hide: you have to talk to this person about the problem. When you do so, try not to be evasive. Look at them, and speak as directly and kindly as you can. Try to identify the cause. There may be a medical reason, in which case you should encourage the person to seek treatment. But even if the cause is self-neglect, it is worth trying to uncover the underlying reason – if the employee will let you.

It is a difficult area, but you'll get nowhere by ignoring it. And don't feel sorry for yourself during the 48 hours you take to build yourself up to the interview. If you want to feel sorry for anyone, concentrate on the person you'll be interviewing. It's much worse for them.

Mental illness

Unlike like the common cold, which we are all able to identify in ourselves and others, the signs of *mental illness* are more difficult to identify, unless they appear in the form of obviously strange, irrational behaviour.

Mental illness is not that uncommon and in some cases may have affected sufferers for many years. The men and women concerned may want to get out and about, viewing daily contact with the rest of the population as some of the best treatment they can get. As a result, they may not feel inclined to reveal their illness to a potential employer. Sometimes their condition will come to light as the result of a protracted bout of absence; sometimes, perhaps, as the result of a failure to maintain normal relations with other members of staff.

There are two points to make. Mental illness is like any other form of illness and must be treated by the employer in the same way. However, it could be grounds for dismissal if the employee withheld the fact of their condition from you at the time of engagement. It has been accepted that a dismissal in these circumstances was fair in a number of cases.

OFFICE AFFAIRS

What is an employer's appropriate reaction on discovering that two of their employees are having an affair? Maintaining that what your employees do in their spare time is none of your business is a perfectly reasonable stance, as long as you're sure that it *is* in their spare time. Your status as employer gives you no special right to act as moral guardian or authority. But if your business is, say, that of running a

incompetence and misconduct

small church charity or something else with strong religious connections, you may be entitled to view the liaison as potentially damaging to the organisation's reputation – likely to be harmful to its business, if you want to put it another way.

If your secretary has a romance with another employee, you may suspect that any hope of confidentiality has gone out of the window. Sometimes certain other members of your staff will express their concern. They may speak of tensions, alleged favouritism, the awkwardness brought about by a particular relationship. They may try to press you hard to 'do something about it', with the implied threat of a withdrawal of co-operation if you fail them.

There's no future in allowing yourself to be bullied into anything. There are a few remedies available, however. If there has been a breach of confidentiality, there could be a case for dismissal, depending on the seriousness of the breach. Your case would be strongest if you had been seen to issue a friendly warning before the liaison started. If the couple had been meeting during working hours, other than in the course of their work, there is another, obvious disciplinary offence.

The tension created within the company, the general atmosphere, is more difficult to deal with. You may try to ease matters by asking the couple involved to be less obvious about their relationship. This may not solve the problem, however. More drastically, you might decide finally that you have no real choice but to fire one or both of the people concerned, if you are faced with the prospect of either a serious decline in morale or endless gossiping. If you arrive at this conclusion, you'd better bite the bullet and be prepared to defend yourself against an allegation of unfair dismissal.

Persuading one or other of the parties to resign is a common solution, but one that you should be wary of. What you see as a simple resignation can become something called *constructive dismissal* (see Chapter 7): resignations are not always what they seem.

MISCONDUCT AND REMEDIES

The Employer's Rules and Procedures – one of the three forms recommended to you – lists examples of misconduct and gross misconduct. This section looks beneath the surface of some of the headings on this form and examines what you can do when there's a need for action.

Instant dismissal

This is more properly called *summary dismissal*. In effect, you will have fired the employee, with immediate effect and without notice. 'Without notice' is essential: if you try to sugar the pill with a payment in lieu of notice, your kindness is likely to backfire. It undermines any justification you might have for your action. Don't do it.

Summary dismissal must, by definition, relate to some episode of gross misconduct. Your actions must be fair and reasonable, and your responses must be proportionate. The same self-testing routine suggested earlier is useful here: would someone impartial, unconnected with your business, regard what you have done as fair and reasonable? Or might they say that a formal warning would have been enough?

There's a second part to this test. Ask yourself: after this offence, will this person's continuing presence at work be wholly intolerable?

The final word is crucial and does not mean the same as the more common 'unacceptable'.

Avoid on-the-spot dismissals if at all possible. They always run the risk of calling your objectivity into question and they are, in any case, unnecessary. Instead of firing an employee or employees here and now, send them home. Tell them they're suspended on full pay for 24 hours, or however long you decide, and that they should come back and see you tomorrow at noon or whenever. By that time you will have had a chance to calm down *and* to make sure that you have thoroughly investigated and understood the circumstances surrounding the offence.

incompetence and misconduct

Just because your employees have been guilty of either misconduct or gross misconduct it does not automatically mean that you can dismiss them or take any other specific disciplinary action without the possibility of rebuke. An industrial tribunal's test will be, here as elsewhere: was the employer's action reasonable in the circumstances?

Criminal charges

An employer is likely to dismiss an employee who has been charged with a criminal offence, if the employer believes that the nature of the offence would bring the company into disrepute by association. It is probably unlikely that the person concerned will bring forward a case for unfair dismissal. If the employer's belief has been arrived at honestly, with reasonable care, most tribunals are likely to sympathise.

Whether the accused is eventually found guilty is irrelevant. Most serious offences take some time to come to trial, and the intervening months provide a period during which considerable harm may be done to the business. Even if the company's reputation is not involved, the employee's work must still be done.

'Frustrating' the contract of employment

While a prisoner is on remand, without bail, it is clear that they cannot work for the employer. To use a legal term, the contract between employer and employee has been frustrated. Frustration implies that the deal struck by two parties cannot move forward because some third party or an act of God, say, or some force of circumstance has prevented it. The rule, however, is that, if frustration is 'induced by either party to the contract', you're not allowed to claim it. In effect, you cannot, in order to avoid going to war, shoot yourself in the foot and get away with it.

You might think that the person on remand has done just this, metaphorically anyway, but this is not the case. The legal argument runs that it wasn't the accused who frustrated the contract: it was the judge, or the magistrate, when they ordered remand.

incompetence and misconduct

There are different classes of criminal offence, of course, and your response will be guided by the nature of the offence. The man who has drifted behind on alimony payments may, if he repeatedly offends, be sent to prison for a short period. If he were to be sent away for, say, 30 days, dismissal might be a disproportionate reaction. Suspension, exceptionally without pay, might be a more reasonable response in the circumstances.

Theft and dishonesty at work

Dealing with the occasional loss of scrap pads, paper, envelopes, pens and so on is no real problem. What about more serious instances when, for example, people help themselves to the petty cash, or bar staff bring their own bottles on to the premises? What about the embezzlers and those whose ambition it is, if undetected, to remove a fair proportion of your materials, stock and tools to their homes?

If you are convinced that what is involved really is theft – as distinct from someone borrowing a power tool to use at home and honestly forgetting to return it on the following day – you may involve the police. If a criminal charge is brought, you are likely to sack the person concerned. But suppose, for whatever reason, the person concerned is found not guilty. Since you have already fired them, is this dismissal likely to be unfair? The answer generally is that it would not – provided that you had acted fairly in the light of the knowledge you had at the time and that you genuinely believed that the employee in question had stolen from you, or done whatever it was that brought about the charge.

There is, however, one important rider to this. You must have given the employee a reasonable chance to explain themselves.

Fighting

There is a common misconception that, provided your company rules say unequivocally that fighting will result in instant dismissal, you are within your rights to take this line of action. Whatever form your rules take, they do not excuse you from acting fairly, reasonably and in proportion to the offence. A tribunal will need

incompetence and misconduct

to be convinced that you investigated and understood fully the circumstances. You must have given both parties to the incident the opportunity to explain themselves. What if one of them was merely defending themselves against an assault? What if this individual, although defending themselves, had nonetheless deliberately provoked the other party?

Fighting should only result in dismissal if you have satisfied yourself that this is the correct, measured response. Incidentally, you are entitled to regard fighting that happens away from your premises, if it is a spill-over from work, as though it took place on your premises. It can be dealt with in the same way – subject to the same need for investigation and explanation.

Drugs

If an employee is incapable of carrying out their work satisfactorily as a result of taking drugs, you are likely to put them on suspension with pay until they are in a fit condition to be interviewed – as you would with someone who was drunk. Similarly, your rules are likely to say that it is forbidden to bring any drugs other than those prescribed by a doctor on to the premises. There's a clear disciplinary offence if this happens.

However, there's a criminal offence here too, even if mere possession is involved. Drugs are illegal substances, and there is no difference between the panel beater smoking marijuana in the corner of the workshop and the young man or woman taking harder drugs during the lunch hour.

Whether the influence is drink or drugs, the person concerned is a threat to themselves and others in the workplace; they are placing everyone in potential danger. You should immediately suspend the employee with pay, decide whether or not to involve the police – and then consider overnight what disciplinary action is appropriate. The options for action include dismissal.

The right to search employees

If you think that the nature of your business demands it, there's no reason why you

incompetence and misconduct

shouldn't include a right to search within your company rules. Should you decide to exercise this apparent power, however, these rules will only give you the right to ask the employee if they will agree to be searched on this occasion. The employee may flatly refuse and be absolutely within their rights. Of course, if you haven't included the right to search within your company rules, you have no such right at all.

If the employee refuses to be searched, you can call in the police – but then, if the employee decides to leave before the police arrive, you've all the makings of a very delicate situation. It is certainly not a good idea to detain people against their will!

More practically, you could argue that, since the right to search was in your company rules, a refusal to permit a search undermined the basic trust that must exist between employer and employee. This line of argument need not imply any wrongdoing on the part of the employee. If you could also say that the employee's refusal eroded discipline generally – because others might join in – there could be a case for strong disciplinary action. But be sure you understand the circumstances properly: circumstances alter cases.

Moonlighting

Moonlighting here means that an employee is working for someone else while working for you, but doing so outside your normal working hours. As long as the employee doesn't turn up for work absolutely worn out each day, you may not mind. If you had not tried to preclude this in your original condition of employment, it will be difficult to prevent it anyway.

But moonlighting has more serious forms. The employee may be working for someone else on your time. Salesmen and saleswomen have been known to be representing two, three or four companies at a time, without the knowledge of the employer who is paying the salary and providing a car. It is not unknown for individuals to set up their own businesses at the expense of their former employer even to the extent of quite deliberately diverting customers.

incompetence and misconduct

This sort of activity clearly amounts to gross misconduct. Assuming that you have investigated the circumstances thoroughly and provided the person concerned with the opportunity to say whatever they have to say, such activity warrants dismissal. Whether or not you decide that it amounts to theft and take the option of dismissal without notice (i.e. summary dismissal) is up to you.

There's a danger in generalising. You might feel some sympathy for the simple soul who had been persuaded by a friend or relative to take a few home-made Christmas cards around in his bag, just in case they could shift them. If your product range is a long way from Christmas cards – who knows? – you might settle for a reprimand.

fair and unfair dismissals 7

INTRODUCTION

Since 1972 most UK employees have had the legal right not to be dismissed unfairly. This right doesn't extend to everybody automatically: for example, people who have been with you for less than two years are largely excluded.

The first step for any employee who believes they have been dismissed unfairly will be to apply for a hearing by an industrial tribunal. Without prompting by either side, ACAS will become involved as a matter of course, in an attempt to conciliate. They will try to achieve a settlement, fairly and impartially, in order to avoid the need for a hearing. If they fail, the hearing will proceed.

Tribunals have decided in favour of the employee in only about one-third of the cases they have dealt with until now. That's not an encouraging statistic for employees. On the other hand, it ought not to persuade employers to play the odds: they're not *that* good.

Who does the right not be unfairly dismissed *not* apply to?

Employees who have been with you for less than two years are not protected by this legislation, provided you did not dismiss them because of:

- trade union membership
- race discrimination
- sex discrimination
- pregnancy.

Dismissal on any of these grounds is always unfair.

Employees who continue to work after normal retirement age will lose the right not to be unfairly dismissed. Conventionally, this happens at age 65, but it could happen

incompetence and misconduct

sooner if your established company policy dictates earlier retirement. Most small companies won't much care, but there's another exclusion in the case of overseas employees. The test depends on where the employee is based, rather than where they live.

Further preliminary considerations

With the exception of the three categories of employee mentioned above, everyone else has the right not to be unfairly dismissed. This sounds straightforward, but it begs three immediate questions:

- Is the person concerned an employee?
- Have they actually been dismissed?
- Was the dismissal fair or unfair?

The answer to the first question is largely a matter of fact, clouded only, occasionally, by the issue of self-employment. It is the issues raised by the remaining two questions that are the subject of the rest of this chapter.

First, how is dismissal defined? Under the law, an employee is treated as having been dismissed in the following circumstances:

- when the employment is terminated by the employer, with or without notice;
- when a fixed-term contract expires, and is not renewed;
- when there is constructive dismissal.

There is seldom an argument concerning the first of these, but some of the less obvious cases are dealt with later in this chapter. The second definition is less easy to fix. Let's take an example. You engage someone on a three-year fixed-term contract. At the end of that period you say thank you, and goodbye. Despite the fact that you have acted according to the terms of engagement, you could still be reckoned to

incompetence and misconduct

have dismissed this individual unfairly, because you did not re-engage them.
There is a way around this apparent craziness. It is possible to write any fixed-term contract of more than a year's duration in such a way as to preclude the individual's rights not to be dismissed unfairly. But the dispensation you get only applies at the full term of the contract, not earlier.

So much for the first two definitions. The third, constructive dismissal, is a more complicated matter entirely.

CONSTRUCTIVE DISMISSAL

If an employee believes you haven't honoured your side of the employment contract bargain, they can walk out, claiming that you have dismissed them unfairly. In more formal language, employees who believe that the employer is in fundamental breach of their employment contract have a common-law right to leave, with or without notice. Either way, this could cost you a lot of money.

What counts as a breach of contract? Cutting an employee's pay by, say, 30 per cent on the grounds that times are hard certainly does. So does telling your salesman that, as from Monday, he must come and work permanently in your stores. So, also, does requiring your workers to transfer to a new location fifteen miles away from the old one, with an infrequent and unreliable bus service. There's a whole range of possibilities. What they will have in common is that the employer has altered the contract of employment with the employee in some *fundamental* way.

In any of these circumstances an employee would be entitled to walk out, without notice, and claim that they had been constructively dismissed through the employer's breach of contract. It won't do you much good as an employer to argue, after they've walked out, that you had made a deal with the employee – that they had agreed to the change, whatever it was. Industrial tribunals almost always take the view that your bargaining position is stronger than that of the employee. So, even if the employee seemed to go along with your suggestion at the time, they can still use the

incompetence and misconduct

constructive dismissal argument, provided they do so reasonably soon after the breach.

Tricking or bullying an employee into resigning is likely to be labelled constructive dismissal. From the employee's point of view however, if they are going to go, timing is important. If employees go along with the altered arrangement for any length of time, they'll lose their right to claim constructive dismissal. In effect they'll have 'regularised' the change.

It is the responsibility of the employee to prove constructive dismissal. As the employer, you do not have to prove the contrary.

NEGOTIATED DEPARTURES

Whenever there is a threat of industrial tribunal proceedings, ACAS becomes involved – they have a statutory duty to try to mediate between the parties at this time. You are likely to be aware of their part in negotiating with large employers and trade unions when there have been national strikes; what you may not know about is their potential usefulness in instances of what might be called *negotiated departures*.

Let's take two examples:

> **Case A**
> Yours is a relatively small company which you have owned for many years. You've got a salesman cum sales manager and you're generally unhappy with him. There's nothing you can put your finger on. His sales figures have slipped gradually away. You are left with that nagging feeling that his 'get-up-and-go' got up and went about a year ago. There's no possibility of using the disciplinary procedure via warnings and so on, because he does just enough to render this approach impractical.

incompetence and misconduct

> **Case B**
> You've bought a business, with an established staff. Six months later you still cannot get on with the woman who is office manager, secretary and bookkeeper rolled into one. You've tried hard, but you and she are oil and water, in spite of a number of heart-to-heart discussions. She doesn't like the way you run the business, and she probably never will.

In each of these cases, you've obviously got to lay your cards on the table. You may find, to your surprise and relief, that the employee feels much as you do. Neither of them could afford to resign voluntarily: jobs are not that easy to come by in the present climate. So what you've got to do now is to come up with a severance package that is fair to both parties.

Going it alone, or involving ACAS?

Let's assume that you have come up with a severance package, and that the employee in question agrees in principle to leave, in return for what you are offering. You might think that all that is necessary is a simple written agreement to be signed by both parties – and there's an end to it. Unfortunately, this isn't the case. The truth is that the employee could sign, take the package and still claim constructive dismissal. Given that the employer is almost always deemed to have advantage in the bargaining process, this is a risk that is not worth taking – so the do-it-yourself agreement is out.

What you should do, instead, is to contact ACAS and ask them to come and talk to you and the employee concerned. The ACAS representative will speak privately to the employee and explain the consequence of agreeing to the deal you have in mind. They will outline any alternative there might be, including toughing it out, if this could be potentially much more lucrative than your offer. If the employee decides, freely, to accept your proposal, the ACAS representative will write out the severance agreement on an official ACAS form, COT 3. Both parties and the ACAS representative will then sign it, and the deal is done. Once the COT 3 form has been completed, the parties to the agreement have no redress: it's binding and final.

incompetence and misconduct

No matter how much you know, like and trust the employee, always get the ACAS agreement signed whenever you undertake a negotiated departure. It's the employment law equivalent of the old saw, 'Put your trust in God: but get it in writing'.

DISPUTED EXITS AND THE INDUSTRIAL TRIBUNAL

Members of the working population tend to know more now about their rights as employees then ever before. And what they don't know they can find out easily enough from any number of sources. This is right and proper, and in theory it is equally true for employers. Unfortunately, however, employers are more likely to act hastily than employees. They'll argue that they had to do something – but, sadly, the price to pay for a rush of blood is usually a trip to the industrial tribunal.

The industrial tribunal

Each tribunal will have a legally qualified chairperson and two lay members, one drawn from the employers' side of industry, the other from the unions'. Tribunals will be found sitting throughout the country on most working days. They operate in an informal manner. There are similarities with a conventional court in the way in which they deal with evidence, although they do not stick slavishly to rules of evidence.

The approach of industrial tribunals is generally workmanlike and pragmatic. It has to be, because the parties appearing before them are not required to use solicitors or barristers unless they so choose. The average employer and employee are perfectly capable of presenting their own argument. As far as the few necessary formalities are concerned, both employer and employee will get the necessary help from the chairperson.

Preliminary procedure

Any employee who believes themselves to have been unfairly dismissed must normally apply to a tribunal within three months, lodging a form called an

incompetence and misconduct

Originating Application. It's pretty simple and will identify:

- the employee
- the employer
- the nature of the claim or the relief sought.

From your point of view – as the employer – the next thing that happens is that the tribunal will send a copy of the Originating Application and invite you to enter a Notice of Appearance. You must complete and return this form within fourteen days.

The form asks you to respond to the employee's claim, which is usually one of unfair dismissal. At this stage, you need only do so in general terms: if you set out the specific terms of your defence, you're stuck with them and will not be allowed to shift ground during the hearing. For example, if you say within the Notice of Appearance that the reason for dismissal was misconduct, the tribunal will not permit you to alter your case and plead employee incompetence when you discover that your first argument is not going too well on the day.

Before you complete and return the Notice of Appearance, consider the following checklist:

- Is this matter so complex that you need external legal assistance?
- Is everyone you need to talk to available? If key people are away on holiday, you might be able to get an extension of time
- Does the Originating Application give you enough to work on? You could ask the secretary to the tribunal to elicit more information from the employee and for an extension – but the tribunal will be annoyed if you use this as a delaying tactic.
- If you think you've no real case to answer, you can apply for a *pre-hearing assessment*. If you get one, both parties will be asked to submit their cases in writing.

incompetence and misconduct

There are two possible outcomes to a pre-hearing assessment: either the employee is told that their cause is pretty hopeless, or the employer is given the same message. In the former instance, if the employee goes forward regardless of this advice, they could – and probably would – get stuck with costs. By the same token, in the second instance, you would be ill-advised to proceed: you'd better settle, as best you can.

The role of ACAS

The ACAS representative will try to settle the dispute between the parties impartially, without the need for a hearing by the tribunal. If this is possible, the agreement reached will be reproduced on the ACAS form COT 3, as was the case with a negotiated departure. As before, it will bind both parties once signed.

You'll do well as an employer to listen very carefully to what the ACAS representative has to say. These people are chosen for their background and experience in labour disputes. This is what they do for a living, so what may be new to you is something they will have seen time and time again. They are always impartial and will offer you sound, practical advice based on their very wide experience. Do not dismiss their views lightly. Even if you win your case at a tribunal, it will have taken up your time. A compromise might be the best outcome for your business in the longer term.

The industrial tribunal hearing

Almost inevitably, however, there will be some circumstances in which an employer will be driven to defend themselves before a tribunal. In this event, spend as much time as possible on preparation: it is not a good idea to imagine that you can just turn up on the appointed day and muddle through.

As the result of your earlier meeting with the ACAS representative, you ought by now to have a clear idea as to the real issues involved. What you had labelled originally in your own mind as a simple combination of principle and common sense may have been crystallised into a matter of fact and circumstance, capable of being proved or disproved in front of a tribunal.

incompetence and misconduct

For your appearance you will need to have gathered together your evidence, and outlines of both the background to the dispute and the disciplinary procedure you followed.

Evidence
Put together the information you have: time and absence records, witnesses' statements, any corroborating evidence supporting your case.

Background
Make sure you've got a copy of the employee's terms and conditions of employment, a copy of the disciplinary code, if there is one, and evidence of their current pay rates.

Procedure
You'll need a copy of the letter dismissing the employee, a statement of your reasons for so doing, copies of any warnings given and any other documentation that has a bearing on this matter.

A final word on the subject of tribunals. At the beginning of this book, you were advised to have a minimum of three forms, one of which was the Employer's Rules and Procedures – the Disciplinary Code, in effect. There's no question that you are better off with it than without it. However, if you've got it, you must use it. It sets out what you require of the employee and what the employee can anticipate from you. The tribunal will expect you to have stuck to your part of the bargain. If you have not, the tribunal, not surprisingly, is likely to react against you. They will refer to what is called a 'lack of procedure'. It speaks for itself. You have to be aware that the bargain you made has two sides.

8 redundancy

THE COST OF REDUNDANCY

Large companies can afford to employ clever people to put a gloss on their less attractive actions. When they make 3,000 people redundant, they are 'right-sizing'; when 50 are involved, they are 'restructuring', and so on. And the employees involved will, at worst, have 'lost their jobs, sadly, by reason of redundancy'.

Whichever way you look at it, what it really amounts to is that these people have been dismissed. The reason was redundancy: the act was dismissal. That should be your starting point. You need to apply the same thought and the same care to redundancy as to any other reason for dismissal.

Trying to avoid the cost of redundancy

If an employee has been with you for any length of time, the cost of a redundancy payment and, say, a payment in lieu of notice, may be very high. It occurred to many less scrupulous employers some time ago that they might avoid part of the cost involved if they could plead that the dismissal involved did not amount to redundancy. They dreamed up all sorts of spurious reasons to test tribunals.

Let's take, as an example of what happened, an employer who moves premises to a new site 30 miles away from the old one. One of the employees, a woman with children at school, finds that it is impossible for her to get to work at the normal starting time and that, at the other end of the day, she will arrive home much later than she judges to be reasonable. In addition, the added cost of travel makes a severe dent in her earnings. She leaves because she feels she has no practical choice.

Her employer would wish to argue that she resigned. If she applied to a tribunal, however, her departure would more than likely be judged to be constructive dismissal, and the dismissal would be deemed to amount to redundancy.

Employers will fail in almost every instance when they use this sort of argument. What emerged from these cases was a cardinal rule that affects every employer.

In any dispute concerning redundancy, it is the employer who must prove that redundancy is not involved. If the employer cannot, it will be presumed that it is.

Is the redundancy legitimate?

The assumption in what has been said so far is that an employee will always want to receive a redundancy payment. If all else fails, this may indeed be true. But there are many occasions on which employees will fight hard to keep their jobs, particularly when they believe either that redundancy has been contrived or that they have been unfairly singled out for this treatment.

So there's an immediate need for a test that defines whether or not redundancy has been created legitimately. The shorthand version is this: an employee is redundant if the whole or part of the business is closed or if it needs fewer people to do the available work.

There's a fuller version, taken from the Employment Protection (Consolidation) Act 1978:

> An employee is dismissed by reason of redundancy if the dismissal is wholly or partially because:
>
> - the employer has ceased, or intends to cease, to carry on the business in the place where the employee was employed;
> - the requirements of that business for employees to carry out work of a particular kind have ceased or diminished or are expected to cease or diminish;
> - the requirements of that business for employees to carry out work of a particular kind in the place where he or she was so employed have ceased or diminished or are expected to cease or diminish.

Employees who are ineligible for redundancy payment

We are dealing with what amounts to an employee's right not to be unfairly dismissed, so the exclusions that have been mentioned in earlier chapters apply here, too. Once again, anyone who has been with you for less than two years will be excepted.

Service before the age of 18 does not count for redundancy payment purposes; neither does service beyond the age of 65 – this applies to both men and women. If your company retirement date happens to be 60, then that is the point at which liability for redundancy pay ceases. But this can only be so when there is no discrimination between the sexes. You cannot use an earlier retirement age for women only in this context.

Payment calculations

Calculating the amount of the redundancy payment rests on two elements: first, a given number of weeks' pay, related to the employee's length of continuous service up to a maximum of 20 years; second, an average week's pay, subject to a maximum weekly amount which is set by the Government from time to time. (Check with your local Employment Service Redundancy Payments Unit for the current position.)

It is no longer possible to get a rebate for redundancy payments from the State. Unusually, if you will be paying an immediate occupational pension to the person concerned, there's a right of offset, but this won't affect the average small business proprietor.

You can reckon the number of weeks involved as follows:

- one and a half weeks for each year of employment during which the employee was 41 or more but had not reached 65 (or your lower pension age, see page 00);
- one week for each year of employment between 22 and 40 inclusive;

redundancy

- one half-week's pay for each year of employment in which the employee was aged 18–21 inclusive.

The phrase 'year of employment' means twelve calendar months. A curious requirement tacked on to the end of these rules involves reducing entitlement by one-twelfth for every month by which someone's age is greater than 64 but less than 65.

Written particulars of calculations

Employers are required to supply a written statement to employees showing how their redundancy payments have been calculated. If you simply forget, you can be fined a substantial amount. If you fail to respond to your employee's written request, it may cost you up to £1,000. However, your employees cannot demand an instant response – they'll have to allow you at least a week to produce your reply.

MINIMUM NOTICE PERIODS

Whether your employee is dismissed as being redundant or for most other reasons – with the exception of gross misconduct involving summary dismissal – you are required to give due notice, or payment in lieu of notice.

The statutory minimum notice periods are as follows:

Period of continuous service	Required minimum notice
1 month or more but under 2 years	1 week
2 years or more but under 12 years continuous service	1 week for each year of
12 years or more	12 weeks

This is the minimum. If the contract of employment you struck with your employee says that they are entitled to more, you must adhere to the contract. If the contract specifies less, hard luck: you're stuck with the statutory minimum whether you like it or not.

SELECTION FOR REDUNDANCY

It is possible for an employee to claim that they have been unfairly selected for redundancy and thus that the dismissal itself was unfair. Tribunals always want to see fair and reasonable means of selection. They'll react badly if there is any indication that an employer is picking on an employee when that employee is apparently no worse than others within the same organisation.

The word 'apparently' in that last sentence is important. You may have all sorts of private – and maybe even very good – reasons for wanting to get rid of someone, but they will not necessarily impress a tribunal. If you want to argue that they are always late, or persistently sick, or that they are thoroughly incompetent anyway, you must ask yourself what on earth any of these things has got to do with redundancy? These are matters you should have dealt with much earlier within your disciplinary procedures.

By the same token, if you see redundancy as providing a neat solution to your problems, think again. If the employee has been with you for some time and there are other, more recently engaged employees doing the same sort of job, the industrial tribunal will not look favourably on you. It could be substantially different if you had gone through the stages of informal and formal warnings and there had been no demonstrable improvement.

Tribunals, or unions for that matter, will rarely argue with the 'last in, first out' approach. There will be times, however, when this is not practical. If you have recently taken on someone with particular skills necessary to your business, you may be much more inclined to shed another employee from the general rank and file. This is sensible. A tribunal is also likely to see this as reasonable, given that the skills in question are real and that they are essential to the business.

redundancy

In the same way, an employer has a clear right to preserve the core of their business, even if a cutback is necessary in the short and medium term. So something called 'bumping' is likely to be seen as reasonable by a tribunal. Suppose you've got a small machine-tool business, and a reduction in numbers is necessary. You may choose to make a skilled operator's job redundant but move the operator into your storekeeper's job for the time being. You then make the storekeeper, who is relatively less skilled, redundant. As a result, you retain the skilled operator, in the knowledge that, when business picks up, you can return him to his old job. You will reason, too, that it will not be difficult to acquire a storekeeper at that time.

For the record, selection will be automatically unfair when it:

- cuts across a specific agreement with a union or the staff;
- is in breach of custom or practice within an organisation;
- concerns a trade union, because of the employee's
    - proposed or actual membership of a trade union;
    - taking part or proposing to take part in the activities of a union;
    - non-membership, refusing or proposing to refuse to become or remain a member of a union;
- is discriminatory on grounds of race or sex;
- has been incorrectly applied to an individual when other employees with the same profile have been ignored;
- is aimed wholly or partially at the dismissal of pregnant women.

You have a duty to talk to your employees about redundancy at some point before it becomes effective. It's common courtesy in any event, but there's another reason. They must have been given the opportunity to draw to your attention skills they might have of which you may have been unaware. It's unlikely in a small business that this will be the case. Nonetheless it is technically a requirement. The theory is that these skills may cause you to think again and to consider redeployment elsewhere.

UNDERLYING REASONS FOR REDUNDANCY

Clearly, if you close a business down, you don't need people to run it any more. And if the volume of work you've now got is less than before, you need fewer people to do it.

Things ought to be that simple, but they aren't, because a tiny number of employers keep trying to bend the rules. There is a comparison here with the Inland Revenue. There are tax experts who dream up tax avoidance schemes to help their wealthier clients. Almost as fast as loopholes are spotted by people trying to bend the rules, the Inland Revenue creates new legislation to close them. The same is true of employment law counter-measures.

Closures

Tribunals will not argue when an entire business closes down. But they might look differently on a business that closed down for a while, only to re-emerge in a re-organised form. If, in its 'new' form, it occupies the same premises and carries on substantially the same work as before, a tribunal might well decide that the closure and re-opening process was a mere device – that the redundancies declared were not real. A tribunal would be capable of declaring them ineffective.

A business might, however, shut down and then surface again in a different form, based perhaps on different technology and skills. Tribunals would be unlikely to argue with this, and in this context the company's renaissance will not help former employees.

Maybe one location among several is being shut down. If the unit is uneconomical, this is patently reasonable. In such circumstances, the employer has a duty to redeploy people, which they may be able to do, if there's another site within reasonable distance. Distance is a key issue here. You can't offer an employee another job at a remote location and argue, if they turn it down, that you've done your bit and there's no redundancy.

Reducing working hours

Be careful about reducing working hours as a temporary solution to the problem of insufficient work. Any significant reduction could amount to a breach of contract and therefore constructive dismissal – which will, in turn, lead to claims of redundancy. If you reduced your working week from, say, 39 hours to 24 and your staff agreed with this arrangement, you could be liable for redundancy payments to all of them. They would be deemed to have been re-engaged, technically, on new contracts of employment based on the revised, lower hours. Your well-intentioned plan to save the company could become the final nail in its coffin.

External sub-contracting

From time to time companies will decide that it makes better economic sense to engage external sub-contractors to do things that were previously done by the employer's own staff. As a result, some of the employer's staff may be declared redundant. It is not unusual for the people involved to be taken on by the sub-contractor, to do what they used to do before they became redundant.

The employer is within the law to take this action. Regrettably, from the employees' viewpoint, the sub-contractor may pay the individuals they take on rather less than their former employer did – but there's nothing anyone can do about it. It's a new contract of employment, freely entered into.

Take-overs

In the majority of cases an employee's rights are protected when a business is taken over. Employees' contracts simply transfer to the new owner, and their service is regarded as being continuous so far as redundancy calculations are concerned.

If the transfer of the business is the reason for the dismissal of an employee – whether this is done by the former owner or the new owner – that dismissal is automatically unfair.

EMPLOYER'S DUTY TO MINIMISE EFFECTS

Redundancy has two nasty side-effects. It puts people out of work, all too often imposing enormous economic pressure on families. And, from the employer's standpoint, it can involve considerable expense at a time when they can least afford it.

As the employer, you will therefore want to avoid the need for redundancy if you can. There's another good reason for doing everything you can to escape the need. If there's a dispute and you find yourself in front of a tribunal, its members may want to look very closely at the way in which you have tackled the problem. They will expect you to have displayed reasonable care in what you have done.

A tribunal has no right whatsoever – curiously enough – to expect you to be a good manager. You have the right to be a rotten manager and to run your businesses into the ground through incompetence or even just because, perversely, you feel like it. But you have no right to behave carelessly or thoughtlessly when you become involved with redundancies.

The following checklist outlines the obvious things you should have considered before you decide that redundancy is the only practical course open to you. There's no law that says you must have acted on all of them, but, if you have ignored them, most tribunals will not look on you favourably. That's not to say that they will invariably decide against you – merely that they will tend to see you as thoughtless or indifferent. These are labels you can do without in any dealings with tribunals.

So before you embark on a course of redundancies, consider the following:

- You should allow for natural wastage. You shouldn't be replacing people who leave of their own accord
- Would early retirement for some people ease the problem?

redundancy

- You should not use temps and casuals when there are potentially redundant permanent staff around
- Recruiting new people might be unnecessary if you can redeploy some of the existing staff
- Short-time working might be possible for a limited period. Take advice, though. Make sure that you do not fall into the trap of creating redundancies, via constructive dismissal, when what you really want to do is avoid them.

9 Useful addresses

Advisory Conciliation and Arbitration Service (ACAS)
(Head Office)
Brandon House
180 Borough High Street
London
SE1 1LW
Telephone: 0171 210 3000
(The Head Office will also provide information about the Regional Offices of ACAS.)

British Insurance Brokers Association
BIBA House
14 Bevis Marks
London
EC3A 7NT
Telephone: 0171 623 9043

British Safety Council
70 Chancellors Road
London
W6 9RS
Telephone: 0181 741 1231

British Standards Institution
389 Chiswick High Road
London
W4 4AL
Telephone: 0171 629 9000

Central Office of Employment Tribunals
The Eagle Building
215 Bothwell Street
Glasgow
G2 7TS

Central Office of Industrial Tribunals
(England and Wales)
19–29 Woburn Place
Russell Square
London
WC1H 0LU
Telephone: 0171 925 5000

Chancellor Formecon
Formecon Services Ltd
Gateway
Crewe
CW1 6YN
Telephone: 01270 500800

Commission for Racial Equality (CRE)
(Head Office)
Elliot House
10–12 Allington Street
London
SW1E 5EH
Telephone: 0171 828 7022
(The Head Office will also provide information about the Regional Offices of CRE.)

your people – an employer's guide to effective people management

Confederation of British Industry (CBI)
(Head Office)
Centre Point
103 New Oxford Street
London
WC1A 1DU
Telephone: 0171 379 7400
(The Head Office will also provide information about the Regional Offices of the CBI.)

Data Protection Registrar
Wycliffe House
Water Lane
Wilmslow
Cheshire
SK9 5AX
Telephone: 01625 545700

Department for Education and Employment
Sanctuary Building
Great Smith Street
London
SW1P 3BT
Telephone: 0171 925 5000

(Scotland)
Scottish Office
Education and Industry Department
Victoria Quay
Edinburgh
EH6 6QQ
Telephone: 0131 244 0615

Department of Social Security
Advice Line for Employers
For basic enquiries about:
National Insurance
Statutory Sick Pay
Maternity Pay
Telephone: 0345 143143

Department of Trade and Industry (DTI)
(Head Office)
1 Victoria Street
London
SW1H 0ET
Telephone: 0171 215 5000
(The Head Office will also provide information about the Regional Offices of the DTI.)

European Commission Representation in the United Kingdom
8 Storeys Gate
London
SW1P 3AT
Telephone: 0171 973 1992
Personal callers 10am–4.30pm
For enquiries about legislation, funding and VAT
Contact your nearest European Information Centre

Employment Medical Advisory Service
At your local Health and Safety Executive Area Office

your people – an employer's guide to effective people management

Employment Service
Porterbrook House
7 Pear Street
Sheffield
S11 8JF
Telephone: 0114 273 9190

Equal Opportunities Commission (EOC)
(Head Office)
Overseas House
Quay Street
Manchester
M3 3HN
Telephone: 0161 833 9244
(The Head Office will also provide information about the Regional Offices of the EOC.)

Federation of Small Businesses
(Head Office)
32 Orchard Road
Lytham St Annes
Lancashire
FY8 1NY
Telephone: 01253 720911
(The Head Office will also provide information about the Regional Offices of the Federation of Small Businesses.)

Financial Times Management
Portland Tower
Portland Street
Manchester
M1 3LD
Telephone: 0161 245 3300

Health and Safety Executive
(Head Office)
Rose Court
2 Southwark Bridge
London
SE1 9HS
Telephone: 0171 717 6000
(The Head Office will also provide information about the Area Offices of the Health and Safety Executive.)

Industrial Society
(Information helpline)
Robert Hyde House
48 Bryanstan Square
London
W1H 7LN
Telephone: 0171 262 2401
(The Head Office will also provide information about the Regional Offices of the Industrial Society.)

Institute of Directors
116 Pall Mall
London
SW1Y 5ED
Telephone: 0171 839 1233

Institute of Personnel and Development
2 Savoy Court
The Strand
London
WC2 0EZ
Telephone: 0181 971 9000

your people – an employer's guide to effective people management

Insurance Brokers Registration Council
Higham Business Centre
Midland Road
Higham Ferrers
Northamptonshire
NN10 8DW
Telephone: 01993 359083

Open University
Walton Hall
Milton Keynes
MK7 6AA
Telephone: 01908 274066

Royal Society for the Prevention of Accidents (ROSPA)
(Head Office)
Edgbaston Park
353 Bristol Road
Birmingham
B5 7ST
Telephone: 0121 248 2000
(The Head Office will also provide information about the Regional Offices of ROSPA.)

Society of Pension Consultants
St Bartholomew House
92 Fleet Street
London
EC4Y 1DG
Telephone: 0171 353 1688